Master of The Straight Line

A Story of Stratton Oakmont

M DETRES

ISBN-13: 9781494232993
ISBN-10: 1494232995

1

THE ROACH MOTEL

ISN'T IT INCREDIBLE how money changes everything? It was never my intent to work in a roach motel. You know, the kind of place where your money goes in and never comes out. I always felt that I was better than that. And it *was* a roach motel. From day one, it seemed that the SEC was just looking for a way to shut us down. And rightfully so. Not because of the numerous SEC rules that Stratton Oakmont violated on a routine basis, but because the firm was the ultimate boiler room. They perfected the art of *pump and dump*. Although the SEC knew it was happening, it was several years before they could actually prove anything.

People might assume that if you were involved in an illegal business, you would want to keep a low profile. Not true with Stratton Oakmont. They had a very in-your-face style, and that didn't sit well with the SEC. The SEC forced Stratton Oakmont to become compliant, at least on the surface. They disliked Stratton's aggressive sales tactics, and tried to make the firm act more like a traditional brokerage firm. Traditional brokerage firms did not pursue customers with cold calls. Unlike Stratton Oakmont, whose average customer lasted three months, traditional firms kept their customers for years.

Cold calling and aggressive sales techniques enabled Stratton Oakmont to become the monster firm that it was in 1994. In that year, America had one million millionaires. I bet my bottom dollar that theses millionaires bought stock. As Frankie always said, "They are all in the market. They all lie. They all buy stock." I knew that I was destined to see some of that action. Imagine me, Ginger Rogers, managing money for total strangers. It was a big responsibility—huge, in fact. How would I ever make it?

In the early '90s, Stratton Oakmont perfected its singular method of opening new accounts. The pitch was based on the straight-line method of sales originally developed by Lehman Brothers, but Stratton Oakmont took it to new levels. The entire room—approximately a thousand brokers and broker trainees—was required to pitch the straight line.

Why? Because it worked. It worked for everyone: male, female, young, old—it didn't matter. It worked.

I set a goal for myself of ten leads per day. I would not leave the boardroom until I met that goal. I was so dedicated to mastering my new career that I spent every waking hour reciting my pitch, my rebuttals, and my closing lines. I would recite the name Stratton Oakmont over and over again during my twenty-minute commute. It had to sound smooth. If I stuttered or stammered when I had a prospect on the phone, the next sound would typically be *click*.

"Stratton Oakmont. Have you heard of my firm?"

"Stratton Oakmont. Does the name ring a bell?"

Stratton Oakmont! Stratton Oakmont! Stratton Oakmont!

I worked late every night, figuring that when the money started pouring in, my husband Freddy would forget those difficult times in our lives and we could move on. I was so very close to the two hundred leads I needed to go on my own. I begged the Bott to let me pitch. I was determined to earn the title Master of the Straight Line.

In 1994, only a handful of female brokers worked on Wall Street. Most of the women I knew would rather marry a broker rather than be one. Understandably, so. On Wall Street in the 1990s, brokerage firms were often aflame with extreme displays of greed—we're talking shootouts, stabbings, window danglings, and the like—related to customer retention battles. I once believed that those things happened only in movies, but I saw all that…and more. When I had the password *bitch* assigned to me, I shrugged it off, realizing that it could have been worse; another female broker had been given the password *slut*.

It was not a place you'd suggest for your wife, girlfriend, or sister as a great place to work. Welcome to my world.

The Wall Street women who survived the brutal environment were typically tough, beautiful, and self-confident, and accustomed to dealing with jerks. They had mouths like truck drivers, dropping the f-bomb at every opportunity. Of course, in the '90s, no one called it the f-bomb; it was just another curse word then. Political correctness? Fuck that shit!

Who would believe that a liberated woman like me would have put up with such abuse and insanity? To understand, it might help to know my customers from Stratton Oakmont—some of the nicest clients I would ever encounter anywhere. All of my customers were gamblers. They had to be. You know the type—the ones who bought stock over the phone, pre-Internet? Although they might tell you a different story, and most guys would not admit it, I knew in my heart that they were compulsive gamblers. They couldn't help themselves. Every broker that worked at Stratton Oakmont wanted to deal with, and actively pursued, the gambler clients.

My customers were the kind of guys who frequented Atlantic City. AC, as we liked to call it, was known as the poor man's Vegas, the place to go if you needed a gambling fix. Customers who opened accounts at Stratton Oakmont were like the obsessive gamblers in AC, with the ability to drop a shitload of money, whether it was on craps or commodities. They loved the high of winning big, and—more importantly—they could sustain the financial blow of losing big without losing sleep.

At Stratton Oakmont, when we pitched customers, we always painted a big picture so that we looked hugely successful. I could talk a big game with such confidence that I was totally believable, even when what I was saying might have been less than forthright. We never lied to customers, per se, but our spin on everything landed us clearly in the gray zone. Of course, once you entered the gray zone, you never left it. We always spoke to clients as though we were investing right alongside them, which I suspected made them worry less and feel better about their gambling. The truth was less comforting.

After I'd been at Stratton Oakmont for three months the Bott finally gave me a copy of the Dr Pepper pitch. He told me to learn the pitch, as well as everything possible about the soda and the company, Dr Pepper. I had memorized many sales pitches in the past, but something told me that this one was different. I wasn't sure what it was, but I was certain that it was a very sexy sales pitch. Perhaps it was because I loved the soda. Or the fact that it was a take-over play. Or maybe it was just that it really did seem to be a wonderful investment. I really didn't know.

I did know that as a hopeless romantic, I had been captivated by one story—apocryphal, as it turned out—that I had heard about how the Dr Pepper beverage had come to be created. The tale claimed that a young, lovesick waiter, distraught over an ill-fated romance with a lovely young lady, had concocted the beverage as a suicide cocktail so he could end it all. The name came from the villain of the story, Miss Pepper's doctor father, who had scuttled the romance.

When you were a broker at Stratton Oakmont, mastering a sales pitch meant more than just memorizing it word for word. The true masters were like artists—some would say con artists—and they had hundreds of apprentices who practiced their skills every day. They painted an irresistible picture of the exclusive world reserved for Wall Street insiders, a world available to only a select few and one that their customers only dreamed about. The great masters would pull the suckers in, tenderly caress them, and convince them that they were close to becoming part of an elite club—if they just bought this stock.

"Trust me," the brokers said.

"I will not let you down," they said.

It took me several nights, but I finally learned to recite the Dr. Pepper pitch perfectly. I knew that I would be great. The biggest disgrace that a Stratton Oakmont broker could face was being accused of letting a buyer off the phone. The company mantra was that on every call, one person was sold: either the broker was selling the client stock, or the client was selling the broker some line, like the idea that he had no money.

"They're all in the market, they're all rich, and they're all lying." That's what we were told at Stratton Oakmont. We only called qualified investors. The strategy of selling small-cap stocks to only qualified investors may have been unique to Stratton Oakmont at the time.

The straight-line method consisted of asking a series of questions that had yes answers, such as "Are you familiar with a company called Dr Pepper?" The first recommendation all Stratton Oakmont brokers offered a client was always a Big Board or a New York Stock Exchange (NYSE) stock. Some called this a bait-and-switch scam, but once again, there's that gray area: Stratton Oakmont clearly spelled out its intent in its "welcome aboard" paperwork, but apparently, no one ever read that crap. So, the first recommendation was always a familiar, if not household, name—and there was always an element of speculation in the recommendation. That's why take-over plays were big.

———— ❦ ————

I will never forget when I called Dr. Ebert for the first time. I pitched him the Dr Pepper take-over play. Dr. Ebert eventually became one of my largest customers; he stayed with me throughout my career as a broker, despite the fact that I never made him a dime!

Here's how it started. "Good morning, Dr. Ebert. This is Ginger Rogers, from Stratton Oakmont. How are you today?"

"I'm well, Ginger. How are you?"

"I'm great, Dr. Ebert. Thank you for asking." We exchanged the usual pleasantries, and then I went right into my pitch. "If you recall, you had a brief conversation with one of my junior staff members, who sent you some information on my firm, Stratton Oakmont. Have you had a chance to review it?"

This opening conversation is a perfect example of how the brokers painted a picture. In the first few seconds of the call, I established that I was a Big Shtocker (as we called them) by casually mentioning that one of my junior colleagues had done the grunt work. I spoke with such confidence that any client would have assumed that I must be doing well.

"I've never seen any information from Stratton Oakmont."

I parried his easy objection. "Believe me, it is right there on your desk!" I said, as if I had personally sorted his mail. I paused slightly for effect, then continued. "Of course, if your desk looks anything like mine, you'll never find it!"

This line always got a chuckle, and Dr. Ebert was no exception. The objection was forgotten. I got right back into the pitch. "More importantly, I've isolated something on the New York Stock Exchange. The *best* idea I've seen in *six* months! A company by the name of Dr Pepper—I'm sure you're familiar with them." I always made the assumption rather than ask if they were familiar with this household name. "The stock is currently trading at $22 per share. My sense, near term…I think we're looking at a $50 stock." Then, to generate excitement, I practically screamed the next line, letting my voice get high and tight at the end: "DO YOU HAVE ANY IDEA WHAT IS GOING ON WITH THIS COMPANY?" *Excitement sells.*

"No, but I suspect that you are going to tell me."

The next step in the playbook was the trial close. "Do this. Pick up a thousand shares. It's a small investment, just twenty-two thousand dollars." Typically, the prospective client would say no. (And anyone who said yes at that point would probably renege.) The no would then be followed by an objection: "I have no money…I'm not liquid…I'm fully invested." Those were the objections raised most often with the trial close—and they were completely ignored, because they were bullshit.

The straight-line pitch was written so that any stock could be filled into the blank—Dr Pepper, Quaker Oats, Apple, whatever. The concept of the straight-line sale was to eliminate all possible objections so that the buyer had no choice in the end but to either buy the stock or hang up the phone. *Buy or die.*

The trial close was just that—a trial. The first *real* attempt came next. "Do you like the idea? Does it make sense?"

With the information I'd given the client at that point, who wouldn't say yes? Again, Dr. Ebert was no exception. Yes! It makes sense to make money! Who doesn't like the idea of making money?

"Well, yes."

Phase one: successful. The second phase of the pitch always ended with the client saying that he thought that the stock would go up. Now, until I called him, it was unlikely that Dr. Ebert had given a single thought to Dr Pepper beyond whether he liked the taste or found himself humming the jingle. So how would I get *him* to tell *me* that the stock was going to go up? Oh, it was so easy. And it worked every time.

"Are you familiar with a man named John Albers? John Albers is the CEO of Dr Pepper. He recently purchased Dr Pepper shares in the open market. He spent $100 million of his own money. More importantly, the British conglomerate Cadbury Schweppes owns a stake in Dr Pepper. Their CEO has *publicly stated* that he'd like to own the whole firm! What do you think happens to the price of Dr Pepper if Cadbury Schweppes buys up the entire float?"

Dr. Ebert was sucked right in.

"It goes up!"

Phase two: successful. "Exactly! Let's go with a thousand shares. I'm telling you! You *will* be very, very impressed." As they told us at Stratton Oakmont, you will never be a successful broker until you ask for the order. Even though

Dr. Ebert was giving me *buy*-signals, he was not ready to give me the go-ahead. He needed to be won over.

"Ginger, it sounds like a great idea," he said. "And I am sure that you are an excellent broker. But I have no money."

I almost groaned into the phone, but caught myself in time. Give me a break! My reply was another Stratton Oakmont standard. "Dr. Ebert, I work on Wall Street. On my way into work, I stepped over a man who was living in a cardboard box. *He* has no money." I heard Dr. Ebert laugh at this wisecrack. Who did he think he was kidding?

Most buyers say no five, six, ten, or twenty times before they say yes. Yet I had found that prospects would usually open an account with me after the third close of my straight-line pitch. That was the phase where I would get my prospects to admit that the only reason they weren't buying the stock was that they didn't know me and therefore didn't trust me. I knew how to deal with that objection.

"Let's say that I had been your broker for the last couple of years, and that I had been making money for you on a consistent basis. Is it safe to say that in that case you'd be a little less hesitant?"

"Yes, Ginger. That's true."

"Okay, fair enough. Obviously you don't know me. But you *do* know Dr Pepper, and in my opinion, Dr. Pepper is not going to zero-bid tomorrow morning. Wouldn't you agree?"

"Yes. I'm sure that you are right," Dr. Ebert replied.

"So, in an effort to make you feel a little bit more comfortable, since you *like* the idea, I'm *willing* to work on half the position. You'll obviously make less money as the stock trades higher, but if you judge me on a percentage gain basis, it will be exactly the same. So let's go with five hundred shares. *I'm telling you*...you'll be a client of mine for life."

By that point, Dr. Ebert, like the hundreds of other clients after him to whom I gave the straight-line pitch, had admitted that he liked the idea, that he thought the stock would go up, and that if he knew me, he would buy the stock, so he had the money. It was the many subtleties in this pitch that made it work.

One subtlety was, of course, the implication that I was right there with him. "Let's go with a thousand shares," I said. Let *us* go. I'm investing right alongside you. We are in this together.

Phase three: successful.

The final close in the straight-line pitch was called Rich Man, Poor Man. "Dr. Ebert. Are you familiar with a stop-loss?"

"Yes, of course." Even if he wasn't, a client might say yes, but it was to my advantage to tell him anyway, so I did.

"A stop-loss is an order to execute a sale at a predetermined price below the market value. Hypothetically, we're long five hundred shares of Dr Pepper. I work a three-point stop-loss on the position. The stock falls out of bed, and I lose you fifteen hundred dollars. Are you going to go on welfare? Is that going to make you a poor man? Best case scenario, Dr Pepper gets bought out, the stock runs ten points, and I put five grand into your account. You're not going to quit your job and retire on the French Riviera, are you? You're not going to get rich…but more importantly for you, you won't get poor either. This will just serve as a benchmark for future business. The only thing I ask is that the next time out, you work in size, and that you send me three of your golfing buddies. That's the way my business grows. Is that fair enough?"

As I said, simple and subtle. I showed him that he didn't have a lot to lose, and he ran out of objections. *Buy or die.* His only option, at that point, was to come up with some bullshit objection or hang up. He tried the former.

"It all makes sense, Ginger. Let me speak to my wife."

Just as in cold calling, I was lightning fast with my rebuttals. "Come on, Dr. Ebert! We're not talking about *furniture* or *curtains.*" He broke out in what can only be called a belly laugh. "I respect the fact that you want to speak to your wife. I'm married, too, and I discuss everything with my husband, as I am sure you discuss everything major with your wife. However, you can be sure that when your wife is in Bloomingdale's buying that $3,000 dress, she is *not* calling *you* to ask for your opinion!"

"My wife doesn't buy $3,000 dresses."

"That's what she tells you! When was the last time you went shopping in Bloomingdales?" I knew that Dr. Ebert would be opening an account with me. I'd heard so many *buy* signals that I knew I had him. It was just a question of time. "So how would you like to title your account? *Individual,* or should we do this *joint* with your wife?"

"No, let's do it individual."

Success.

He was worth the fight.

———◦◦◦◦———

I learned to not care about anything. I became a schmoozer. I developed my bullshit rap and took it to a new level. My whole shtick had actually started many years before, at a time when I had been totally dedicated to fashion. When I landed a high-profile job in the fashion industry where buyers looked to me to predict trends, I had to learn how to speak with confidence.

In the past, I had always been afraid of being wrong, and ended up trapped in place by my own analysis paralysis. Then one day, I was asked to forecast a trend, and it dawned on me that what I was being asked for was only a projection. Typically, I had a fifty-fifty chance of getting it right. Since most stores bought months in advance, it was unlikely that when shoppers did or didn't prove my prediction right, buyers would remember me specifically and what I had forecast as a trend.

It turned out that the most important aspect of design forecast was not *what* I said, but *how* I said it. If I spoke with conviction, people bought my bullshit! They believed me. A light bulb went on in my head and a salesperson was born. *If you are in sales and you master this one concept, you will be successful.* Even in other parts of my life, when I spoke with conviction, people believed me and would buy what I was selling.

The guys at Stratton Oakmont got that, which was one reason why they were wildly successful. They understood the importance of selling with conviction. Their training often included instructions on how to generate excitement because, as they said over and over, *excitement sells.* When you get excited, customers want to know "What the heck's going on over there? What are you selling?" They figure that it must be something great because you are excited about it.

One reason I was successful was that when I was determined to succeed at something, I was unstoppable! For example, take my job searches in the fashion industry. When I saw an ad for a head designer position at a major apparel firm, I wasn't at all worried about the fact that I had not been working in the industry for years. No: I looked at the ad for a senior designer, and I thought, *I can do that.* And since I had just graduated from the Fashion Institute of Technology with a degree in fashion design, I was certain that they would be very impressed. It never occurred to me that by *senior* they meant that they wanted an experienced designer—not someone fresh out of school.

Most people have a vision of clothing designers as creative artists who devote their waking hours to sketching the latest fashions. Many designers, and I include myself in this statement, cannot draw well. To compensate for my lack of skills, I worked on developing my sales techniques. It didn't take me long to discover that my calling was not in design but in sales. I was selling all the time. I sold myself, my look, and my vision constantly, whether I was working with a buyer, being interviewed, or showing a line to my sales reps. If I could not sell a clothing line to my salespeople and get them excited, how could I ever expect them to sell the buyers?

I had a lot of natural sales talent, which I built on while I was in fashion. But I really honed my skills when I went to Wall Street. At Stratton Oakmont, we were trained on everything, and especially sales. It was really unbelievable. The masters at the firm truly walked trainees through the process. I didn't understand then that the program was especially designed to create Strattonites who were loyal to the *family* and who would do as they were told without questioning the process.

If I'd thought about it more at the time, I would have realized that Stratton Oakmont was selling me, too. I had learned the lesson that it's not what you say but how you say it, but in those early days, I took the training at Stratton Oakmont at face value. For example, they trained us how to handle the price guarantee. It was completely illegal to guarantee the price of a stock. The SEC came down hard on price predictions, so Stratton Oakmont trained us to use a work-around. By adding a few words, they said, we could imply a guarantee with what was legally just a prediction. We would never say that a stock was going to hit a certain price; we'd preface our would-be guarantees with wishy-washy qualifiers like "My sense is that this stock could…I think we might be looking at…I believe we could have…" And the only part of the sentence that the customers really heard was the second part that said "$50 per share."

Changing our pitch to add the work-around only helped fuel my belief that at Stratton Oakmont, we were trying very hard to be SEC compliant. But what it could also have taught me was that Stratton Oakmont was going to earn pots of money, and it wasn't going to let the SEC or anyone else stand in its way.

———————

How did this happen to me? How did a good girl from Long Island get involved in this mess? What was really ironic was that since the initial trade was always a Big Board stock, the first trade usually *did* work out well for the customers. If clients never bought another stock from us, they usually did okay. However, that was not the how we played the game. If customers didn't buy our recommended stocks, we generally told them that they weren't suitably committed to be Stratton Oakmont clients, and suggested that they close their accounts. Imagine that!

Stratton Oakmont was, on the face of things, very concerned about its brokers being compliant, but the training was all just a show for the NASD (National Association of Securities Dealers). Stratton Oakmont didn't train people to become better brokers; because of the ongoing SEC investigation, the firm initiated a training program that instructed the brokers on how to be compliant with SEC regulations. The SEC objected to the use of sales scripts, the way that brokers seemed to guarantee stock prices, the aggressive way they sold stock—even how the desks in the office were arranged—and Stratton Oakmont agreed to make changes. But the firm never changed its basic strategies, or its mission to make money, and lots of it. And why would they? What they were doing was working, and if they needed to keeping making adjustments here and there to slither between the lines of the law, so be it.

Stratton Oakmont's style tested the laws that governed securities and laid the groundwork for the aggressive sales techniques that many other firms later adopted. Here's a great example of the Stratton Oakmont style: The SEC banned the Stratton Oakmont office in Baltimore from selling a new issue because that office was not licensed to sell IPO's in Maryland.. Frankie tried everything possible to convince the NASD regulators that Baltimore should be given an exception because…well, actually, God knows what he said. He probably made up some bullshit reason. The NASD totally shot him down, which isn't surprising; they really didn't like his style. Frankie was so furious that he flew every broker in the Baltimore office to New York; from there, they called their Baltimore customers to offer the stock. As you can imagine, that in-your-face strategy was not very popular with the SEC.

Everything at Stratton Oakmont was designed to cover the owners' asses, especially because of the ever-present scrutiny of the regulatory bodies. One reason I thought that Stratton Oakmont was making a serious, major effort to be compliant was that the SEC had agents in the office for weeks reviewing everything we did.

Frankie used to warn the brokers during his daily brainwashing pitches that life would be harder for us if we left the firm and went to another firm. Frankie said no one would protect us like Stratton Oakmont did—what we needed protection from, he didn't say—and promised us the firm's support. "We're behind you all the way. We'll pay your legal fees." That was probably intended to sound reassuring.

Legal fees? I could not imagine the law coming after me, but Frankie never seemed to worry much. When he heard that a customer wanted to sue him, he said, "Sue me? Tell him to stand in line! I've got a whole floor of Jewish lawyers that will rip his face off." He wasn't kidding. I didn't realize at the time that it really was not normal to anticipate being sued. I thought that it was simply the nature of the business. It seemed to me, at the time, that the large number of lawsuits directed at Stratton Oakmont was probably typical for the industry, and no different than and exactly the same problem that doctors battled. The average doctor in the 1990s faced a constant barrage of medical malpractice suits. How was this different?

The concept of Stratton Oakmont was a brilliantly executed plan. We only dealt in speculation. It was like the Bott often said: "The stock market is the world's biggest casino." We only dealt with wealthy businesspeople. We were only allowed to deal with financially qualified, experienced investors; to qualify for an account at Stratton Oakmont, a client had to have a net worth of $1 million or greater, and annual income of at least $200,000. Customers were also required to have had experience investing in equities, with a minimum account value of $100,000. Believe me, no one wanted a customer who was a piker— someone with less than $100,000 in the market.

The concept was such a setup. When clients cried, "I lost all my money!" there were so many built-in rebuttals: "You told me that you were an experienced investor. You knew the risks involved. You only lost a fraction of your net worth. You know there are no guarantees in the stock market."

Unfortunately, I found out too late that those replies wouldn't stop clients from suing our asses off. *Buyers are liars.* Especially buyers who have lost money.

Especially buyers who have lost *all* their money.

Some people say that I am a real person, and that I really was once a broker at Stratton Oakmont in the '90s. Others say that Ginger Rogers is a fictitious character, a composite of multiple brokers, disguised so the tales I tell will protect the innocent…and the guilty. The name invokes a time of innocence and hope. I knew exactly what I was doing when I worked at Stratton Oakmont. I was struggling to survive.

This story is dedicated to every woman working on Wall Street.

2

BBQ

W HEN I THOUGHT about my life at any given time, I thought of myself as a missile. I know this image is incredibly phallic and erotic. Maybe if I had a penis, it would be an easier concept for others to swallow (there I go again). But the image has always felt apt. I always focused on my target, took aim, and fired. When I wanted something, I wanted it *now*. I never gave up. I was described as persistent, relentless, and (my favorite) a die-hard. When I made the decision to possess something, I became a different person—as if I were the one possessed. I had to have it. End of story.

My thoughts on competition were simple: *I can't stop until I win.* For me competition was strictly binary; it was about winning or losing, and I hated to lose. I was all about instant gratification and winning. What was the point of playing if I didn't play to win? For as long as I could remember, I had wanted one thing. I was not just driven; I was obsessed. I wanted my fifteen minutes of fame, and then some. I wanted the glamorous life of the rich and famous. I wanted to be a famous sought-after clothing designer!

Wall Street? When the guided missile that was me was trained on Paris and Milan, Wall Street might just as well have been Siberia. It was certainly someplace foreign to me in March 1982, though I was still living in Manhattan at the time. That is, my husband Antonio and I were living in Manhattan—specifically in a two-bedroom apartment in the West Village, just north of Houston. That blustery day I had left work at lunchtime and gone home. I was three months pregnant, feeling fat and constantly exhausted, and I just needed sleep. I had just gotten cozy in bed when I heard a knock at the door, followed by the ring of the doorbell.

Feeling enormous and sluggish, I lumbered toward the door. I reasoned that it had to be a neighbor, since ours was a secure building, and I suspected it was the annoying artist from next door. She had learned that I was a designer, and had started treating me as her personal art supply store. I prepared myself to politely but firmly send her away empty-handed.

When I opened the door, I was facing two uniformed NYPD officers. "Ma'am? We're looking for Ginger Rogers." *What the fuck did Antonio do now?* In a New York minute, my life changed forever. "Are you Ms. Rogers?"

"It's Missus, thank you."

"Yes. Mrs. Rogers. The super let us in, told us where to find you, that you were pregnant. Your husband is Antonio Rogers?" *What the fuck did Antonio do now?*

"*Yes.* What's up, Officer?"

"Your husband was shot this afternoon while walking down Second Avenue in the East Village," he said. "We're sorry to have to tell you this. He's dead."

I was so stunned that I could not talk. I have no recollection of the rest of our conversation, although I know they gave me more details about what had happened, and where his body was being held. The moment they left, I called my family and told them between loud sobs what had happened. They immediately jumped in a car and headed to Manhattan to take me home to Long Island. All the way home I thought about how lucky I was that my parents lived so close, and that I still had both parents. My unborn child would not have both parents, only me. And Antonio's parents...

"Oh my god! I've got to call his parents!"

I believe that my father-in-law answered the phone, but I don't really remember. I do recall that the sounds of their screams and sobs over the phone reminded me that while their only son may have been a fuckup, he was *their* fuckup, just as he had been *my* fuckup. And he was gone. Forever.

I was just fifteen when I first met Antonio. I was at Herricks Pond, a dinky little man-made drainage pool that had been turned into a public park. We kids just called it The Pond. It was a patch of green tucked next to the intersection of two fairly busy roads. It was the summer of 1970, and girls like me, those who wanted to smoke pot and meet boys, went to The Pond. I loved the place, and hung out there often, but that was the first time I'd seen Tony there. I had noticed him in school on occasion, but had never had the nerve to go up to him there. What senior would bother with a lowly sophomore? Ah, but The Pond was the great equalizer. And that day, I caught him looking my way. He was *so* good looking…I felt my knees start to buckle. Nevertheless, I did fancy myself a rebel, so I walked over to him.

"Hi!" I said.

Antonio, with his charming smile, said, "No, I am not high. Well, not yet. Would you like to smoke a doob with me?"

Duh. I was never one to refuse a good doobie. I looked at Tony. Our eyes met for a brief couple of seconds. *Wow.* "Sure," I said, trying to disguise the fact that in just ten seconds I had fallen so hard for the guy that I was already imagining myself as his girlfriend.

"Cool." Tony reached into his pocket and took out his stash.

One moment I was marveling at the smooth, light olive skin of Tony's sinewy arms, and the next I looking down at those same arms sporting a glinting pair of handcuffs.

"You are under arrest for possession of marijuana." The two narcs had materialized out of nowhere, and before I could say a word, they had led him away. When I reminded Tony of that day many years later, he laughed. He said he hadn't even known my name, but he had always remembered me as the beautiful girl who was there when he got busted.

Returning to the relative quiet of my parents' house, combined with the harsh realization that my husband had died a brutal, violent death, made me realize just how difficult it would be to raise a child as a single mom—especially in Manhattan, which was rapidly becoming a city that consisted of only the super wealthy and the really poor, with the middle class being slowly squeezed out. I could not see myself as a single mother anywhere, but especially not there. I was not super wealthy, but living on my own with a newborn while trying to work full time to pay the bills…I just couldn't imagine it.

So, even though I hated the thought of becoming part of the BBQ crowd—the people in Brooklyn, Bronx, and Queens—I moved to Great Neck on Long Island. Though I later came to regret selling my apartment, at the time I was thrilled to have made $100,000 profit from the $130,000 sale: it had two bedrooms and a large living and dining space, but it only had one bathroom and a tiny kitchen. Of course, fifteen years later it would have sold for more than a million dollars, but at the time I had more pressing, much more short-term concerns. Just a few months after I moved to Great Neck, Tony Jr. was born.

After Greenwich Village, the move to Great Neck was culture shock. I felt like the only shiksa who lived there. If I came home late, the town was deserted. Where were the people? Why were the stores closed? In Manhattan, on those summer nights when it was still so hot and humid at two o'clock in the morning that I couldn't sleep, I could still rely on my favorite remedy, retail therapy. Bored? Go shopping! Lonely? Go shopping! Hungry? Go shopping!

One of the brain's neurotransmitters, dopamine, controls our pleasure-seeking impulses. It plays a huge role in addictive behavior, and drives people to continually pursue things that will make them feel good. For some, that may mean drugs. For others, that could be gambling—or playing the stock market. For me, it meant shopping.

Living in Great Neck put a serious crimp in my reliance on retail therapy. Of course, I had another problem that didn't help with that: I was always broke. Even though I had sold my Manhattan apartment and made a quick hundred thousand, I never seemed to have any money. Reality check: some people might find it hard to sympathize with my crying poor when they understand that I was not a bargain-store shopper. Fashion was my passion, remember? I didn't just go to Bloomie's now and then. No, I went often. And I went shopping in London, Paris, and Rome four times a year!

I was shocked to learn that the best-dressed women in the world were not found in Manhattan. They did not live in London or Paris. They lived in Great Neck. If you wanted to see the hottest fashions in the world, hop on the 8:05 from Great Neck to Manhattan any weekday morning. That particular Long Island Rail Road train should have been called the Garmento Express. It showcased a truly mind-blowing display of wealth and decadence. Fittingly, Great Neck had some of the best and most exclusive stores on Long Island, but the women who lived there did not shop there. They would *never* pay retail.

When the discussion turned to money (and it always did), I could never compete with anyone who lived in Great Neck, nor with anyone where I worked. However, having money was never a problem for a beautiful woman. Most of the women I worked with could not compete with me when it came to looks. I didn't want to hang with that type of woman anyway. That's why I never had any real friends. Most women didn't want their husbands near me, and I didn't blame them, although I was not at all interested in *any* of their husbands. I found their weak, miserable spouses pathetic. They weren't even rich or good-looking. Why would Sweet Ginger waste her time with men who had no control over their sexual desires?

⁕

Although I still remember it as though it happened yesterday, it was 1975 when I first met Bill Levine. I had just walked into the showroom of The Right Bank on my way to an interview with the company's president when I was startled to see a buyer that I knew. Not only was he someone that I knew, but we had recently crossed paths when he had shopped the line at my current company. I was terrified that he would alert my employer that I was thinking of leaving. I turned my face away and tried to regain my composure.

To shift my focus back to my main objective—get the job!—I studied my surroundings. The company was in a less-than-prime location, 1350 Broadway. The premiere buildings for sportswear were both on 1407 Broadway and 1411 Broadway, although true garmentos—Garment Center employees—never bothered to say the street name. They just said 1407 or 1411. That said it all.

I was pleasantly surprised, therefore, by what I found at 1350. The space itself was very modest in terms of size, and yet there was a lavishness about it that made me feel empowered. It had most likely been professionally decorated, and quite recently, but mercifully without using any of the unfortunate colors that were so popular in the '70s. The carpeting was a wool Berber in the palest shade of gray that worked beautifully with the four round steel tables. Sleek, contemporary black-upholstered chairs were strategically placed, for privacy, along the wall with the view—and what a view it was! The Right Bank was located on the twenty-third floor, with a clear view of the East River. It was breathtaking. It was by far the most professional showroom that I had seen.

In an era of cost-cutting initiatives, where an English-speaking reception-ist was considered a luxury, I was thrilled to meet Bernice, who operated the front reception and switchboard. I could sense that I was in one of the most important firms in n New York—one that not only influenced fashion locally but also impacted trends globally. It was the type of company that dictated to all what they should wear and how they should look.

I noticed Bill Levine's sensuality when I first met him.

It was a Friday, but the East Coast had not yet adopted Casual Fridays. Bill walked into the showroom wearing the crispest white cotton shirt I had ever seen. I made a mental note: instruct dry cleaners to use heavy starch on Antonio's shirts. Bill's thin summer-weight wool pinstriped pants had to be custom-tailored. They were fitted without being tight, hugging his butt and bulge in a way that was both subtle and yet suggestive about exactly what was hidden away (yes, he wore it on the left side). He completed the sophisticated look with a silk designer tie.

I loved seeing a man dressed like that. It turned me on. Although I was still quite young, however, I was professional. And I was there for a job inter-view, not a date. In any case, I was somewhat intimidated by Bill's good looks and obvious charisma, and I was fairly certain that the man, who was married and much older than I—at forty-three, he was ancient by my standards at the time—would not be interested in me anyway. In fact, at the time I wasn't really interested in him in that way so much as I was just very, very impressed...and determined to impress *him*.

I was beautiful, but I also had skills. I wasn't much of an artist, but I had an innate sense of style and an intuitive knowledge of developing trends. To me, that meant I deserved to be paid big bucks. I shifted from appraising his physical attri-butes to gauging what I would need to say to Bill Levine so that I would be hired. After all, The Right Bank was his company. He would make the final decision.

I wanted to make not only a good impression, but a lasting impression. Although most fashion designers are employed on average by a firm a year, that was not my style. I am a long-term player. (This is especially true when I am in love.) When I had dressed for my interview that morning, I knew that I needed something that would transition seamlessly from daywear to evening wear, as I planned to go out later that night and party with some friends. My interview was scheduled for just after lunch.

I chose my favorite wrap dress. Not just any wrap dress, but my Diane Von Furstenberg wrap dress. Her slinky print wraps of curve-hugging jersey, especially animal prints like the one I wore that day, had transformed basic sportswear into career-wear…and date-wear. Since Diane had married Prince Egon von Fürstenberg in 1969 and in so doing had become Princess Diane, the dress made me feel like royalty (dare I say a JAP?). It lent me exactly the right amount of self-confidence that I would need to get this job.

Of course, it couldn't hurt that I looked hot and I knew it.

I had heard some gossip that the owner of the firm was a player, and I was determined to use every asset I had to get the job. My dress was cut low enough to show maximum décolletage, and wrapped tightly enough to accent my tiny waist and hips. I wore my four-inch black heels, carried a black clutch and my slim portfolio, and I felt ready. When I saw the elegant space—and Bill Levine—I was glad that I had decided to splurge on the DVF wrap dress. Even at wholesale price, the dress had cost me a small fortune, an expense I could hardly afford as someone still fairly new to the workforce. Although I could probably write off the dress as a job-hunting expense, the truth was, I just loved it and would have bought it regardless. The black and white zebra print was cut from the finest silk jersey fabric, a fabric that required highly skilled hands, so it had been sewn in Italy.

"Ginger Rogers? It's really nice to meet you," said Bill, with an appraising look. I could see that my presentation efforts were not wasted on him. "Great name, by the way."

"Thank you."

"So, I can see from your résumé that you are a recent graduate of the Fashion Institute of Technology. Summa cum laude—very impressive," he continued. "I also see that you are currently employed by one of my competitors, and that you have been there for just three months! Why are you looking to change?"

Of course, I was prepared for the question. "Although they are lovely, lovely people, they are not always very…professional. Whereas I can tell that *your* company is a first-class organization." That was my diplomatic way of explaining that my current employers were potheads who kept their office doors locked because they were always inside banging different buyers every chance they had. Bill Levine just smiled. It was obvious that he knew.

I could feel it then, some crazy chemistry between us, and I felt more determined than ever to get the job. I was glad that I had decided to wear my long strawberry-blond hair in an elegant up-do rather than let it go wild as I normally did. The day was terribly humid, and the up-do gave me a sophistication that certainly did more for the image I was trying to convey than if I'd walked in with my typical high-humidity frizz-bomb. I hoped it made me look confident, though not arrogant. I was a woman on a mission.

After reviewing my portfolio, Bill looked me up and down again. "I'm looking for someone with experience. All you have is a degree."

I was prepared for this objection and had practiced my rebuttals. I looked directly into his eyes. "Take a look at the way I'm dressed," I said.

He knew I was right. He had devoured me from head to toe as soon as I'd walked into the room. Something about me, though, seemed to cause him hesitation. I was definitely turning him on, and yet he seemed almost scared.

"You're too young to know what you're doing. Yes, you have an impressive degree. But designers like you are a dime a dozen. You're just a little too young," he said. "I run a $20 million company. I might consider you for an *assistant* designer position, though, so I hope you will come back to me when you get some experience. My designers have been in this business for ten, fifteen years."

I kept my voice steady and level, and smiled when I answered. "And that is *exactly* why you need me," I said. "What I can offer you is a young fresh look— something that you are not getting from your *experienced* designers."

He paused, then stood and extended his hand. When he shook my hand, he intentionally held it just a little too long. I looked deep into his beautiful brown eyes. When our eyes locked, I felt warmth in them that I had never felt from Antonio. Just when I sensed that Bill was growing uncomfortable, I turned and walked away. I could feel his eyes burning a hole in my back, into my soul, as I walked slowly out of the room. It took all my courage not to say another word. I instinctively knew what I would later be taught at Stratton Oakmont: After you go for the close, the one who speaks first loses. I was already around the corner, so I could not make out exactly what he muttered as I left, but it sounded a lot like "Goodbye, Ginger Rogers. I will see you again."

Round one winner: definitely Ginger Rogers.

I had felt good about the interview, so I was not surprised when I eventually got the job. I was surprised, however, that several months had gone by before I heard from Bill Levine. He didn't call me back immediately, as I had expected, so eventually, I called him. I started my job campaign by calling Bill once a week. Then twice a week. Then every day.

I had not had any formal sales training at that point, but I worked with a man I considered a mentor. Neil Hautz made really good money and was a great role model for me. I especially loved the way Neil pursued his buyers. He was relentless. He absolutely hammered the buyers to get them into the showroom—in a nice way, of course—and I used his lessons on the power of persistence.

When I was finally hired by The Right Bank, Bill admitted that he had offered me a job just so that I would just stop calling him. Funny the things that you remember from years ago.

I spent twenty years in the Garment Center. Then I was ready for a change.

3

THE INTERVIEW

I HAD NEVER before answered a blind ad for a job, and the whole concept seemed rather strange, but I had found the ad in the *New York Times*, so it was most likely legit. The company was looking for a stockbroker trainee. I suspected that my résumé would be thrown out as soon as Barry Bottsworth saw my work experience, so I was shocked when they called me to come in for an interview. Normally, I wouldn't even have considered going on an interview without knowing at least the name of the company, but those were not normal times. In normal times, someone with my talents could not have dropped out of the fashion industry, where she had commanded a six-figure salary, and find herself applying for a trainee position at minimum wage. I scheduled the interview, sure that I would be laughed out of wherever I was going. Stockbroker trainee? I had no background in finance.

I had no idea what to expect. Although I was reasonably sure I didn't stand a chance of being hired, I felt compelled to go since I had not worked in months. I had also had to reschedule the interview once before. Stratton Oakmont was located in a typical business park in a suburban bedroom community that was actually part of the city of Great Neck. My husband Freddy and I had just closed on a house in Port Washington, not far from Great Neck, which we had decided on because of its easy commute to Manhattan. For New Yorkers, a one-hour commute is considered easy, a great commute.

Of course, there was a certain cachet to living in a place with a long history of being associated with wealth and power. Long Island had many estates and mansions that reminded you daily of the famous families who not only lived there but were instrumental in building this great country: the Vanderbilts, the Astors, the Whitneys, and the Morgans, all had huge estates there. John Lennon had an estate called Strawberry Fields there. They had all been drawn to Long Island for two obvious reasons: one, its proximity to New York City, which, in my opinion, is the greatest city in the world; and two, its incredible natural beauty. From Long Island's South Shore, known for fabulous white sand beaches to the North Shore's Gold Coast.

With its incredibly beautiful landscaping that covered its shores. Port Washington, part quaint fishing village and part yuppie mecca, was a dream come true for me. When Freddy and I were able to pay just $265,000 for our adorable hundred-year-old fixer-upper, we were thrilled!

Freddy's job at AIG paid most of the Port Washington bills, but we were flirting with foreclosure on the ski house that we owned in Vermont. Not that I really cared; I hated that house anyway. It was a dive. Freddy and his buddy Dick had bought it during the real estate boom of the '80s. It was so poorly constructed that I could imagine the original owners laughing their asses off all the way to the bank when they heard that a couple of lame New Yorkers had bought the place sight unseen.

That's right: sight unseen. Who does that? Okay, it was a vacation house, not a full-time residence. But seriously, how busy could they have been that they felt unable to make a four-hour trek to Mount Snow make sure the place even existed? Apparently, just busy enough. Then Dick got married, and found that he could no longer afford his half of the mortgage payments. Freddy and I were stuck with the $150,000 shack.

"Freddy, maybe we should sell the ski house?" He gave me one of those looks that said, "Do not go there," as though the place was like a part of his manhood. I had to admit that it did sound rather satisfying to tell our yuppie friends that we had a five-bedroom ski house in Vermont. I agreed that we should keep it, but vowed that the minute we had the money to renovate it and turn a profit, it would be gone. I especially hated the Yuppie Puppy poster there, and could not wait until it met its maker (also known as the trash).

When I told him that I was worried about how we could pay for both houses and still maintain the extravagant lifestyle that we were so determined to live, Freddy, always the optimist, just laughed. "Come on, Ginger. What are you worried about? We will find a way. We always do. I think it's exciting living on the edge!"

At that moment, we had twelve hundred dollars to keep us from falling off the edge.

I sold the painting I had inherited from Uncle Al to Sotheby's.

Even making the Port Washington expenses wasn't always easy. Everything was expensive in Port, as the locals called it. It had the finest restaurants, bakeries, delis, boutiques, and everything that money could buy. Our bills were beginning to pile up. Freddy's salary was good, but not good enough. I had no choice. I had to go on this interview. I had to make some money. I had to find a job that would allow us to continue to live a more comfortable distance from that edge Freddy loved living on.

It didn't seem at all strange to me that a large brokerage firm would be isolated in a run-of-the-mill suburban office park. What did feel strange, almost fated, was that the part of Great Neck in which the office park was located was called Lake Success. The drive in my Z4 from my house in Port Washington to 1979 Marcus Avenue in Lake Success would be just fifteen minutes on an average day.

The blind ad might have been for a trainee position, but it promised to pay a $100,000 salary…and it was close to home. There had to be a catch.

The day of my interview was *not* an average day. Long Island is regularly subjected to such extreme weather conditions that residents have to learn to adapt to drastic climate fluctuations. Long-time Long Islanders grow accustomed to hundred-degree-plus summers with high humidity, and winters where the landscape becomes an unforgiving, wind-whipped frozen tundra. In recent years, the area endured everything from minor earthquakes and tornados to devastating hurricanes and blizzards. So far, it had been spared a plague of locusts.

Had I lived somewhere else, I might have taken a look at the weather that day and called to reschedule the interview. But I had been living on Long Island off and on all my life, and I didn't frighten easily. I had also woken up with the first signs of one of those god-awful stomach viruses, the kind of bug that hits you on both ends. Freddy was just getting over it, and my kids were in the middle of it, so I knew what I was in for, but certainly I could make it through one morning before it really hit me.

Freddy was wrapped up in the comforter on the bed, still looking slightly green. He could see by the bedroom windows that the snow was really starting to come down and the wind was picking up. I hadn't even told him about the ominous gurgling sensation in my stomach. "Ginger, honey, you're not seriously considering going on this interview? I mean, come on, what are the chances that you'll get this job? Slim to none?"

"You're probably right, Freddy," I said. "And I would rather spend the day in bed with you and the baby. But I can't cancel the interview *again*. That would kill any chance I might have of getting the job."

"Yeah, I know. But look out there! I worry about you driving in the snow, Honeybuns," he said. "And what about the kids?"

"Oh, Freddy. You're so sweet. What's a little snow to an intrepid New Yorker like me? I'll be careful. I promise," I said. "And I'll probably be back before the kids even wake up. Their fevers are gone, but they were both up most of the night and I think they'll probably sleep all day. Check on them in an hour or so, though."

I knew that I had to go. Honestly, I wasn't too thrilled about the fact that it was snowing outside. No, let me clarify that. It wasn't just snowing; it was a raging blizzard. But I had to go. We really needed a second income, and the $100,000 was just too enticing to pass up. The most difficult part was dragging myself out of bed. Our century-old house had three tiny bedrooms upstairs and one first-floor bedroom. It was perfect for us for our family: each of the boys had his own room, and the spare was used for the housekeeper.

We'd taken the first-floor bedroom, into which I still couldn't believe we'd managed to fit our massive bed, an old oak four-poster that I'd dressed up with antique gold curtains to gave it an exotic, inviting look. I'd seen walk-in closets bigger than our room.

I crawled out from under the down comforter and stood in the narrow space next to the bed looking down at my honey. Freddy was burrowed deep into comforter so only his face peeked out. He was adorable. He watched me dress. "Please be careful driving. You know how I worry about you."

"I'll be fine, Freddy," I said. "It's just down the road, and I'll be extra cautious." Had I been honest with him, I was a little worried about me, too. It was only a fifteen-minute drive to Lake Success in good weather, but this was the opposite of good. My car was not at its best in snow, so I decided to take Freddy's Z-4. Although his sports car was not great on ice, I looked really hot in it and that was all that mattered to me. And as often happens with drivers who imagine that they are skilled in the snow but actually have very little experience driving in it, I had not properly honed my bad-weather driving skills. At least I'd had the good sense to leave a full hour early for the interview, but even that proved inadequate given that when traffic moved at all, it barely moved fast enough to register on the speedometer. It would be an understatement to describe my first trip to Stratton Oakmont as treacherous. Perhaps I should have seen that as an omen.

I did finally make it to Lake Success, and to the parking lot for the office park. I was feeling more than a little queasy by then, so even though I was running late I sat behind the wheel for a few minutes to gather myself. The building itself was barely distinguishable from a thousand other business parks—just a three-story arrangement of brick and glass surrounded by a large parking lot with the usual sad bushes and spindly trees in a few median strips. But there were two things that seemed out of the ordinary. One, the parking lot was surprisingly full for such a foul-weather day. And two, the parking spaces were not filled with what I would have called typical business and professional cars. I was not really a car person, so obviously what I was seeing had to be unusual for me to notice, and it was. I was surrounded by the most amazing collection of exotic and expensive cars that I had ever seen in one place: Porches, Beamers, and Mercedes were everywhere, and even closer to the building, several Ferraris, a Lamborghini, and a Bentley.

What the hell went on at Stratton Oakmont? I wondered, as I took the infamous glass elevator up to the second floor (or maybe the third). I say infamous because I found out many months later that the elevator was a favorite place for Stratton Oakmont brokers to get laid. Imagine fucking in a glass elevator. (I'm not gonna lie; I found the idea pretty exciting.)

The reception area for Stratton Oakmont was nothing like I had imagined after seeing the parking lot. No mahogany desks, no leather chairs—not even a Persian rug or an Oriental vase in sight. There were none of the traditional signs I would have expected from a successful financial firm. I even wondered if I was in the right place. If the people there were making money, they were not flaunting it like so many of the in-your-face yuppie nouveaux riches I'd encountered lately. Or so I thought then.

I stepped over to the receptionist. "I have an appointment with Barry Bottsworth."

The woman behind the desk barely glanced up from her computer. I would have thought she was hard at work had I not been able to see the reflection of computer solitaire in her glasses. "You can have a seat over there while you get started on the paperwork." She handed me a clipboard of papers and a pen.

After completing the required forms, I handed them to the receptionist and returned to my seat. My complexion, which was naturally pale, was so white from the drive and the flu that I could have sworn I heard the receptionist announce to Barry Bottsworth that Casper was in the lobby.

While I waited, I resumed practicing my smooth answers and polite rebuttals to the questions I assumed he would ask. I was confident that I was as ready as I possibly could be for an interview for a job I knew nothing about. Finally, Barry Bottsworth waddled in. Although he was average in height and looks, there were two things that caught my eye immediately. First, he had a *huge* gut, especially for a guy who looked to be in his early forties, and second, he was wearing one of the most magnificent suits that I had seen in a long time. I later learned that the big producers at Stratton Oakmont had their suits custom-made by a tailor who catered to them at the office. Leave it to me to pick up on that little detail.

I was impressed.

He held out his hand. "Nice to meet you, Ginger. Barry Bottsworth, managing director. Everyone calls me the Bott," he said, motioning me to follow him. We sat in a small conference room with cheap plastic chairs and a beat-up table. "Any problem finding this place?"

"Huh? Oh, no. I live close by." Did he know that there was a blizzard outside? Finding the place had been easy. Seeing it had been much more difficult.

"I see from your résumé that your experience is mainly in the Garment Center. What brings you to Stratton Oakmont?"

That was one of the few questions I felt truly ready to answer well and with complete honesty. "Well, Barry, I started as a designer, but my real talent is in sales. The only people who make money in the Garment Center are the owners and the people in sales."

He made a little squiggle on my résumé and asked, without looking up at me, "How much money are you looking to make?"

The ad had said that the trainee position paid $100,000, so I knew I could ask for at least that amount, but I didn't want to lock myself into anything. "At least six figures."

The Bott was still not giving me a lot of warm and fuzzy eye contact. I was getting the sense that he had already written me off as not good enough for the job, but was wondering how else he could use me and profit from my inexperience. He continued to make mysterious marks on my résumé. I was sure that this was going to be the shortest interview of all time.

"And why do you want to be a broker?"

I was not sure what to say. I really had no good answer prepared, so I went with the obvious. I thought about *Wall Street* and *Glengarry Glen Ross*. "It sounds exciting, and I know it pays well."

I saw by the expression on his face that I had said the right thing. I felt like I was on a game show. I was waiting for the bells: *ding, ding, ding—good answer!* And like any game show contestant, I just kept telling myself to try to relax and get to the next level. Just get through the interview. Just…just…don't throw up. I took some deeps breaths, and that old missile mentality flared up inside, propelling me forward. Maybe it was my somewhat nauseated state or my financial worries, but despite the little warnings and red flag—the low-budget reception area, the isolated location, and the fact that they were even talking to me—I shifted back into competition mode. It was all about not losing. I would not lose my chance.

The Bott finally looked up at me. "Do you remember the company Tiger Jeans?"

"Yes, of course," I said. "Who doesn't?" Every garmento had heard of that big moneymaker.

"Ginger, I was the owner of that company. I closed it three years ago because I felt that I could make more money here," said the Bott. "You'll meet a number of folks here who worked in the Garment Center." Again, my instincts should have warned me away. He was trying to sell me on the job, not the other way around. But as much as I wanted the job, in my increasingly infirm state, I was already starting to fret about the drive home, and thinking that the longer I wasted my time wasting *his* time, the worse the weather—and my flu—were bound to get. I was getting ready to thank him for his time and make a run for it when he said the magic words. "You're right, Ginger. It's very exciting, and it pays very, very well. That hundred grand is just a low estimate, you understand."

Only later did I realize why Stratton Oakmont was located twenty miles from Wall Street, had an armed security guard at the door, and didn't spend money on a lavish conference room, boardroom, or reception area: they wanted to *discourage* customers from ever visiting the office or meeting their brokers in person. Most brokers at Stratton Oakmont never sold to local customers so they could avoid the dreaded "drop-in" clients. As one broker put it to me later, "Do you think I want some irate customer to come storming in and shoot me in the fucking head?" No, the policy was pretty clear. *No need to stop by. Just send us your money. Send all of it.*

I thought of the cars outside. "The parking lot has a lot of—"

"Like that Bentley? That's mine," said the Bott. "And I'm telling you now, I didn't buy that when I owned Tiger Jeans."

It pays very, very well. Stratton Oakmont brokers were making money. A lot of money—enough to buy Bentleys and Lamborghinis. And unload tumble-down ski shacks. It was exactly the type of opportunity that I had been looking for. The upside could be unlimited! It might have been the fever setting in, but it was intoxicating. The lure of the green sucked me right in. All logic went out the window. One thing was clear: the owners of Stratton Oakmont had figured out not only how to get their brokers hooked, but how to keep them loyal and motivated. It worked. It worked very well.

Now that it seemed that I actually had a chance of getting the job, I started to worry about how I could possibly remember all the bullshit I'd lay-ered into my résumé. It was going to be a sitcom-style interview: one person lying about the past, and the other lying about the future. It didn't matter, though. I was so thirsty to win I was ready to drink the Kool-Aid. I wanted that job. I could see myself working there: Ginger Rogers, the Baddest Bitch on Wall Street. I wanted it all, wanted everything I imagined, had seen in the movies, and read in the papers—the money, the drugs, and the whole Wall Street world.

I was like one of the tourists I often saw in Manhattan playing three-card Monte. That's a slight-of-hand gambling game: the con would usually use two black cards and a red one, place them face down, and bet that the mark couldn't pick out the red one. The con would start out by turning over the cards to show the starting point of all three so that the mark would know, or think that he knew, which one to follow, then the con would shuffle the three cards back and forth, over and under, so fast and so many times that would be impossible to keep track of the red card. The con might let the mark win one or two hands to encourage bigger bets, but even though the game might seem like easy money to the tourists, the marks would *only* win if the con set it up that way. The tourists in New York—probably everywhere—found it impossible to resist, even when they suspected, or even knew, that they were being cheated. It was so hard to walk away from easy money.

I was the Stratton Oakmont's mark that day.

The Bott gave me his version of that famous line that from sales training. "We hire a lot of fresh talent. But there's a 90 percent chance that in six months, two of every three of the people we hire will be gone."

Ooh, a direct challenge. My years of working in the Garment Center had given me the chutzpah I knew I would need to not only survive life in that secret society, but to thrive in it. I would find those numbers were rather optimistic for Stratton Oakmont, where the turnover was especially high, but all I could think of at that point was that I would be the one who made the cut. I would be a winner.

I learned later that inquisitive applicants were encouraged to "get the fuck out!" In addition, anyone who had worked in another brokerage firm before and knew the business need not apply. Stratton Oakmont wanted to hire inexperienced, uneducated schmucks with dollar signs in their eyes. In other words, me! Sure, I was a college graduate, but I was a know-nothing when it came to the financial world. I had no idea what the Big Board was, and to me over-the-counter had to do with nonprescription drugs, not stocks. In 1994, only government and academic types had access to the Internet, and the web as we know it today did not exist. It was not possible to hop online and read about a company. For that, people had to rely on the library, magazines, or newspapers. Because my father worked for many years as a staff writer for the *Daily News*, I was well aware of the fact that newspapers had their own political biases, and that sometimes things that got published weren't fact-checked or in any way established as true. When I walked into Stratton Oakmont on that miserable day, I knew nothing about the firm. I didn't even have the company's name. When I responded to the blind ad, I was simply given the address and suite number before the interview.

In retrospect, if I had to name the number one characteristic that the owners of Stratton Oakmont valued in a new hire, that would be loyalty—even blind devotion. Frankie Porter, the head dude, was obsessed with the mob. He spent hours watching movies like *The Godfather*, *Scarface*, and *GoodFellas* over and over again, like training videos. Stratton Oakmont controlled its staff by paying them very well and giving them the sense that they belonged to a secret, very exclusive club, like a family. Not *the* family, but better: the Stratton Oakmont family.

Stratton Oakmont was run like the mafia, and the Bott would be *my* godfather. He stood up from the worn conference room chair and motioned for me to follow him. I scooped up my purse, certain I would not be returning. We walked a short way down a hall.

"Let me show you the boardroom," he said. I was expecting a large room with chairs grouped around a table, perhaps something slightly grander than the drab, poorly appointed conference room we'd just left. I was completely unprepared for what I did see.

The Bott pushed open the door. I was peering at about ten thousand square feet of raw energy compressed into an otherwise nondescript space. The room was laid out in a basic grid, with rows upon rows of desks, each with a phone. Every other desk also held a Quotron, a terminal linked to the outside financial world and stock prices. They gave the only clue that the massive call center belonged to a brokerage firm.

The shades in the few windows in the room were drawn, probably to keep the brokers from being distracted by the storm. It appeared to be working: the entire room seemed oblivious to the raging blizzard. It felt like being in a casino, where after a while there is no sense of time. That was fitting, since the Bott often called the stock market the biggest casino in the world. He was wrong about that: at least in a casino, players had a chance to win. It was not a *big* chance, but it was a chance. At Stratton Oakmont, all bets were rigged; the house never lost. Never.

In the front of the room, there was a large whiteboard with several names written on it. Somewhere near the middle of the room was a wide aisle that separated the front of the room from the back. Poles equally spaced along the open aisle suggested that a wall had been opened up to enlarge the space. There were half a dozen private offices on the side of the room. It was obvious that the action was in the front of the room.

Even though the back half of the room was laid out exactly the same way as the front, although without the Quotrons, it did not generate the same energy. There was a whiteboard with names in the back, too, off to one side.

This was nothing like I had imagined. A bunch of cheap desks crammed together? Where were the mahogany desks and corner offices? No cube farms? No privacy? I *loved* it. I was sucked right in. It was intoxicating.

I couldn't help noticing how few women there were in the room. Before me were several hundred good-looking young men, most of them standing, shouting, and literally pounding the phones. The excitement in the room was overwhelming. I had never seen anything like it before. I was sure that this must be exactly like working on Wall Street. Later—always later—I learned that Stratton Oakmont was the epitome of a boiler room brokerage, and sneeringly known as a roach motel: once the money went in, it never came out.

The Bott and I walked through the boardroom for several minutes as he explained the setup. "The way it works, Ginger, is really simple. When you start at Stratton Oakmont, you begin as a broker trainee. The trainees are the ones sitting in the back. As a broker trainee, you will assist the broker in obtaining *qualified* leads," he said. "After a month, you begin training to pass your Series 7. We will sponsor you. When you pass your test, you will become a licensed securities representative. The firm is looking for brokers, not cold callers. It is in our best interest to get you licensed as quickly as possible."

Even though all the brokers and the trainees were busy working their phones, their eyes still followed the Bott and me as we toured the space. I felt hundreds of eyes looking me up and down, making me uncomfortable. I felt like I was on parade, or being appraised at an auction. My first response was close to anger—this is *bullshit!*—but then inspiration struck. I reached inside for Ginger Rogers, Queen of Dating, and gave anyone who dared to locked eyes with me a seductive look. I stared back until they blushed or looked away. I won

— 35 —

the room over instantly. My initiation parade would *not* be a walk of shame; mine was the sweet Ginger walk of game!

We stopped in the middle of the large boardroom. The Bott stood in the aisle that separated the back of the room from the front. He slowly turned to face the front of the room and spread his arms out. "This is where the magic starts," the Bott said. "Once the broker trainees pass the Series 7 exam, they get to move up front with the licensed securities brokers. See that whiteboard?

How could I miss it? It was like a movie screen at the front of the room.

"The names on the whiteboards acknowledge the top brokers and broker trainees. Those are the ones who can get ten leads in a day. And if you can get ten leads in a day, you can be rich."

Rich. I liked the sound of that.

The Bott motioned to one of the few female brokers in the room. She stopped what she was doing and trotted over. As she held out a manicured hand, her diamond tennis bracelet slid up her arm and disappeared behind the cuff of her silk shirt and the sleeve of her Armani suit. "Laura Ferraud," she said.

"Laura has been with us for quite a while now," said the Bott. "I'm sure she'd be happy to answer any questions you might have." He walked away and engaged a young broker in a conversation that I felt certain was completely for my benefit, to give Laura time to grill me. She looked more than capable of weeding out the people who couldn't cut it, and I hoped I could sell her on my winning personality and sales skills.

As it turned out, she was there to sell me. "Ginger, if you have any doubts about this job, let me tell you: coming here was the best financial move I ever made," she said. "I feel very lucky to have joined the Stratton Oakmont family. They have been so wonderful. I'd never done anything like this before—and I was a dental hygienist for years!—but they walked me through the program, and trained me every step of the way."

"Really?" This was great news, considering I didn't know the Big Board from Big Bird. I figured I should just be direct. The fact that I was still trying to get through the morning without hurling emboldened me. "How much did you earn last year, Laura? Two hundred grand? Two-fifty?" I had never worked with people who were willing to discuss what they earned, ever, so I was shocked to find that it was apparently part of the culture at Stratton Oakmont.

"Gosh, no, not quite that," said Laura calmly, not at all offended. "I haven't even been here for a full year yet, so I only made about $185,000. But I have to say that my bank account for a woman my age is substantial."

I may have been drooling at that point. I do know that I never expected to meet a former dental hygienist younger than I who was bringing home big bucks and wearing earrings that looked like they could pay all my bills for a month, including both mortgage payments. Stratton Oakmont had me exactly where they wanted me at this point. I took the bait hook, line, and sinker. Hell, I was ready to jump straight into the boat myself.

The Bott and I left the boardroom, and not a minute too soon. I felt dizzy and my stomach was filled with butterflies, probably from a combination of the flu and the thought of all that money. The Bott guided me back to the reception area, stopping near the rack where I'd hung my coat on the way in. My spirits sank as I realized that he had walked me to the door, not his office, and was about to send me away.

He held out his hand, and as I shook it, he said, "So, Ginger, are you available Monday?"

"Excuse me?" Maybe there was hope! This sounded like a second interview offer.

"Ginger, I can tell that you're the kind of person who knows how to hold a job," he said. "I'd like to offer you a position as a broker trainee. Can you start on Monday?"

"Start...Monday?" It was Friday. I hoped this was only a twenty-four-hour bug! If not, too bad.

"Trainees start out at rock bottom, $250 a week. But after six weeks of training, you get your Series 7 books," he said, smiling. "Once you pass the exam, there is no limit to the amount of money that you can make."

Suddenly I began to worry. Six weeks at $250 each...that wasn't going to help much. And how long after that would it be before I could pass the exam? And what if I was *never* able to pass it?

The Bott seemed to be reading my mind. "I can tell that you won't be satisfied making $250 per week. And that's the point: we don't want that. We aren't looking for permanent cold callers," he said. "The position we need to fill and the only one that is available is for a registered rep, a licensed securities broker. We want someone with the drive to transition to a broker position as quickly as possible. It should take you about three months."

Three months…a thousand bucks a month…my head was spinning, trying to figure what bills we could juggle, where we could cut back for just a little while…

But the Bott wasn't finished. "At Stratton Oakmont, we don't put a cap on your earnings like other companies. Here, the sky is the limit. If you're willing to work hard, tune out all the distractions, and put your nose to the grindstone, in three months you can be rich."

I hesitated. I wanted to say yes, but although I was the one who was worried about money, I wanted to talk to Freddy first. It just seemed like the right thing to do.

"Ginger, I have faith in you. I'll tell you what. You go home and think about it, talk it over with your husband, whatever. If you decide *not* to take the job, call me on Monday. But if you decide you want to be rich? Just show up here Monday morning at seven thirty, and we'll get you set up and on your way."

I left Stratton Oakmont feeling totally beaten up. Not by the interview—I'd gone through more rigorous application processes as a teen looking for part-time jobs at the mall. But I was growing seriously ill by that point, and every bone and muscle in my body ached. The good news was that the storm had scaled back to just occasional flurries and random gusts of icy wind. The bad news was that the temperature had plummeted, and the roads covered with slippery snow over a layer of ice. After a white-knuckle drive that included a 360° as I tried to make the turn onto our street, I finally edged into our driveway in Port Washington.

Freddy met me at the door. He hugged me, gave me a sweet kiss, and helped me off with my coat.

"Hey, Honeybuns, how did it go?" He looked prepared to console me.

I went into sales mode. "Great! I met with the managing director, this big fat guy in a gorgeous suit. Barry Bottsworth. He absolutely loved me!"

Freddy kissed me again. "Who could blame him? What's not to like? So… tell me more! What did he think about your résumé? Was he worried that you don't have a background in finance? Did he ask you for a second interview?"

"No…he offered me the job," I said, walking toward the bedroom to change.

"Wow, already? That's fantastic!"

"I'm a little shocked myself. I was only there for about a half an hour, and most of that was spent on the tour. It's weird—I mean, who does that? Who hires somebody on the spot after talking for just ten minutes or so?"

"Well, it's a trainee position, right? So all they care about is that you are trainable. What's the pay again?"

"That's the thing. I didn't tell them I'd take it yet because for at least three months, I'll only make two-fifty a week. There's an exam I have to pass, this Series 7 thing that allows me to sell securities, and then it all comes down to what I can sell, you know?"

"Woman, you were *born* to sell, and you know it," he said. He was helping me undress.

"I am pretty good at it," I said, hanging my suit in the tiny closet. I sat down on the edge of the bed.

"Ginger, you could sell condoms to the Pope," he said.

His enthusiasm was reassuring. That made me feel better. Freddy was obviously feeling a lot better, too, as he was continuing to undress me.

"Where are the kids?"

"Still sound asleep, poor things. I checked them about ten minutes ago and they're both flat out. We've got a little time all to ourselves to…celebrate."

My Freddy was adorable. I think he was more excited about the job than I was. The thought of making a lot of money was like an aphrodisiac—for both of us. Suddenly, I really wanted Freddy. "Give it to me, baby. I missed you all day." I whispered to him. Dirty talk always turned him on. "Put that hard cock in me, now."

He pushed closed the door, stepped to the edge of the bed where I was sitting, and pushed me back, and we had crazy wild sex—*mugambo* we called it between ourselves. "Harder…harder!" I cried. "I need to feel you, all of you…OH yes, right there…!" My words turned into tiny squeaks and moans as Freddy put his hand over my mouth to muffle my sounds of joy. We exhausted ourselves, and finally just collapsed on top of each other and fell fast asleep. The last thought I remember having was that our lives were about to change and become even more wonderful than before.

It was late in the evening when I woke up. I heard Freddy puttering in the kitchen, and found him making soup and toast for the kids. He took one look at me and could tell that the flu had finally hit me, so he sent me back to bed with a mug of peppermint tea and a handful of aspirin. I lay propped up on the luxurious mountain of pillows and closed my eyes, drinking in the scent of our wild afternoon. It had been wonderful, yet perversely I found myself remembering a night from many years before.

I was in a limousine, being driven home from the World Trade Center after *the* most fabulous Christmas party ever. Of course, it would have to have been, since it was hosted by the hard-partying, reckless, rich man who owned the company—and who sat next to me in the back of the limo. Bill Levine.

I looked stunning. My strawberry-blond hair, worn in my airy Janis Joplin frizz like a glowing corona, was working its seductive magic. Since the dress code was more relaxed in the banquet hall than at the famous restaurant, I arrived Manhattan style—twenty minutes late—wearing a Norma Kamali cat suit layered with a long black and silver blouse. I was a true New Yorker: we will always wear black until something darker comes along.

Maybe it was the moonlight, or the thousands of tiny lights twinkling everywhere in the winter night—along the streets, in the trees, across the city, in the sky. Maybe it was the warm, satisfying afterglow from the festive party and delightful food, and the feeling of finally being where I belonged. Maybe it was the five glasses of Cabernet I'd downed rather rapidly. Or maybe it was Bill's hand between my legs. Whatever the reason, it felt to me like the perfect night for a romantic tryst.

Until that night, we'd shared only smoldering looks and the briefest, careless brush of fingers on bare skin. It was a bad idea and I knew it—he was married, I was married, he was my boss—but I was a beautiful young woman with a skewed sense of entitlement. Bill and I had never spoken of what we obviously both felt, but that night I could sense that there was no more holding back…that our passion was about to explode like a broken water main in the middle of the night.

It started out innocently at first, or at least it would have appeared so to any curious coworkers. Bill offered to drive me home so we could continue our conversation about the new merchandise manager to whom I reported, Gene. I gave Bill's driver my address in the West Village. He nodded, and the privacy screen went up.

"That flamer, that fag you made my new boss? His beautiful brown eyes are that color because he's so full of *shit*! Nothing's ever his fault...he'll lie right to my face and tell me I got an order wrong when everyone knows damn well he fucked it up because he's such an emotional train wreck!"

"Ginger, please. We never use the word 'fag' at The Right Bank. And I know you don't like him because he's immune to your wiles, but have an open mind. He comes from St. Germaine Couture. His knowledge and experience are already proving to be tremendous assets for us."

"Ass-ets! Ass-ets! He's so frickin' jealous of how well you and I get along that I'm surprised he hasn't tried harder to get me fired so he can get his *ass*-ets closer to yours and—"

I suddenly found my diatribe against Gene stifled by Bill's tongue in my mouth. I forgot about Gene as Bill's hand began searching for an opening in the cat suit, meandering and probing, and it felt wonderful. I wanted more, so much more. I wanted him, I wanted his money, I wanted his lifestyle, and I wanted his dick. I really wanted his dick. Bill knew he could have me: his wife would look the other way if she found out about his infidelity. She always did.

Bill found his opening. Literally. His hand worked the soft, wet lips that welcomed him while his mouth worked mine. He kissed me so tenderly and passionately that I lost control. My orgasm was so intense that even if we'd gone further that night, it could not have been better. But although within moments of my coming we were both more naked than not, things derailed. Seconds before he was about to penetrate me, he whispered, "You know Ginger, I will never leave my wife for you. Although I care deeply for you, I am not in love with you."

I sat up. "You bastard."

He sat up, and said nothing.

"Is it because I'm not Jewish?"

Although I was crazy for Bill Levine, for me, it was over. Just like that. He was Jewish. Leaving his wife for a shiksa would have been a huge disappointment to his daddy—a mistake that his brother Bob would soon make. Apparently, Catholic girls were for fucking, not marrying.

I learned a valuable lesson from that brief encounter with Bill Levine: Beware the garmento!

The next morning, I walked into the Right Bank and resigned.

So much for my career in fashion. It was time for a change.

———— ⨭⨭ ————

The day after my interview at Stratton Oakmont, I put in a call to my old friend and sales mentor, Neil Hautz. He and I had remained friends, but even when we were both single we had never hooked up. Neil was divorced and never seemed to have gotten over it; I think he was still looking for a clone of his first wife, the quintessential nice Jewish girl. On paper, Neil was now the president of the apparel manufacturer where we had once worked together. When the firm started to have financial problems, I was let go, but Neil had stayed on. I knew that he had been toying with the possibility of leaving the Garment Center and working for a brokerage firm, so I decided to call him for advice.

"Neil, did you ever follow through on that brokerage thing you were considering?"

"Ginger, tell me you aren't getting out of the business!" he said.

"I answered an ad for a trainee broker position, and I went to this interview…'

"Ah…stockbroker trainee, $100,000, no experience required?"

"Yes! That's the place. Did you interview there?"

"Yes, Stratton Oakmont. I interviewed there about two weeks ago,'' he told me. "The owners are all former garmentos who couldn't make it the Garment Center. Then they started this place and now they're making a shit-load of money."

"So…what…you took the job? Are you working there now?"

"Nah, I need a change that'll get me away from the phones for a while," he said. "I'm thinking about forensics." Typical Neil. He loved the extremes. "Tell you what, though. I was sold. I just put my money with them. We've only done one deal so far, but I made some good money." That was all I needed to hear. Not exactly due diligence, but I trusted Neil. He wouldn't steer me wrong.

The next day, Sunday, I got a call. "Hey, Ginger, how ya doin'? This is John Bufano from Stratton Oakmont," said the oily voice. "The Bott asked me to call and thank you for coming in on Friday. He's looking forward to having you on the team."

"Well, I haven't actually joined it yet, John."

"I'm shocked! What's not to like?" he asked.

"I'm not gonna lie, John. I want to say yes, but just $250 a week for at least six weeks—"

"Oh, I hear ya," said John. "What do you think it'd take to get you in there on Monday? Three hundred? Three twenty-five?"

I saw my chance and I took it.

"Three fifty is the bare minimum that I'd need to survive," I said.

"You're tough, Ginger. A negotiator. The Bott loves that," said John. "He can do three fifty. I'm sure he'll kick in the extra hundred each week in cash himself, if he has to. So, Ginger, welcome to the team. See ya at seven thirty on Monday."

And that was that. The sooner I started, the better, I figured, so I could pass that Series 7 and get on with it. I might have been leaping into a different industry, but even that major change in my life didn't really scare me. I had worked for so many different companies in my life, and at every one, I had found the same bullshit. Wall Street would be no different.

It wasn't…and yet it was. I had no sooner walked through the double doors into the boardroom and found an unoccupied spot in the first row of trainee desks when a man burst into the room and halted in the exact center of the room—about ten feet from where I had just sat down. Tall, impeccably dressed, and grinning like a madman, he looked like an older, more refined, and more manic version of my late husband Antonio. He walked to the nearest Quotron and heaved it as far as he could throw it toward the back of the room, then stalked to the front of the room and started methodically erasing names from the massive whiteboard. He whirled to face the brokers, shaking his arms over his head like he clutched an invisible pair of maracas.

"You guys are the *laziest* pieces of shit I have ever, ever seen!" he shrieked. His voice was high and thin. "You *cannot* sit around waiting for a new issue! We have *unbelievable* buying opportunities with *all* of the companies that we're recomending! You guys are a bunch of piker midget *assholes*! I…am…so…*sick* of hearing you guys *whine*. Pick up the phone! Pick up the fuckin' phone! It's not easy, but it's *sooooooooo* simple. Your customer calls and complains that his stock is down? Tell him to buy more! When do you *want* to *buy* it, Mr. Customer, when it has *doubled*? You need to buy stock *every* day regardless of what the market is doing. If the market goes up, you buy stock. If it goes down, you…buy…stock.

The *worst* thing you can do is *nothing*. That's paralysis by analysis. The bulls *and* the bears eat." He turned and walked out of the boardroom and closed himself up in his private office and hit the *play* button on his VCR .He needed to finish watching The Godfather for the third time this week.

It was five minutes past seven thirty on my first day at Stratton Oakmont, and I had just attended my first come-to-Jesus meeting, hosted by none other than Frankie Porter, one of the owners of Stratton Oakmont.

I was speechless.

At seven forty, the man from the phone, John Bufano, gathered me and nine other new hires into a tiny room with metal folding chairs, a pair of cheap tables, and a row of coffee pots next to a battered old refrigerator. John and a pair of older brokers launched into what they might have considered a pep talk, but that felt like a watered down version of the screeching we'd just been subjected to in the boardroom.

"Cold callers? Scum of the earth. There's nothing lower. But without the information you guys dig up—you make sure that the brokers are only call-ing qualified prospects—nobody gets rich. If the clients don't have money, we don't make money, got it?" They let us get coffee, although after my first sip I resolved to start bringing a thermos from home. Expensive suits, cheap cof-fee—that was Stratton Oakmont. The ten of us sat on the hard metal chairs without saying a word.

I had been called many names in my past, but scum of the earth was a new one. I had also worked in some pretty cheesy settings, including one company where available space was in such short supply that I stood in the hall all day designing clothes. But this...this was quite a rude awakening.

John introduced us to Anna Keller. I believe he said she was the office manager, but whatever her title was, I began thinking of her immediately as Frau Keller, as she seemed ideally suited for processing papers at a Nazi con-centration camp. That first day, I thought her absolutely horrible, and it was only after working there for several months that I started to understand her complete lack of interest in seeming the least bit human. The churn rate at Stratton Oakmont was so high that she was like a war-weary senior officer on the front lines, the kind who gives up on learning the ever-changing names and faces of the foot soldiers and starts thinking of them as nothing more than numbers, knowing they would probably soon be leaving in body bags.

Frau Keller looked at us with a strange expression. If her face hadn't seemed to be made of stone, I would have called it a smirk. "Welcome to Stratton Oakmont." She slapped a thick stack of papers in front of each of us. "You will sit here and fill out these forms. You will have the forms back in my office by nine o'clock, or you will be sent home. You will bring them to me with two forms of picture ID, or I will not accept them. You will have your fingerprints done by Wednesday."

Where had they found that bitch? I found it extremely hard to take this woman seriously, but I could see that the threat to send trainees home would be effective: hours away meant docked pay. I knew that I needed every penny of that pathetic paycheck, and I could tell by my fellow rookies' reactions that they did, too. Being sent home was not an option. So, we all put up with abusive Frau Keller—and her very bad breath. It smelled like something had died in her mouth.

In a different life, Anna Keller might have been pretty. She was tall and thin, and wore her long bleached-blond hair in a ponytail held back with a bow, a look that she had most likely developed decades earlier and never abandoned. If she been dressed in a black leather jacket, jackboots, and a peaked cap, with a black leather gloves and a rawhide whip, she would have made the perfect Nazi Barbie. I could picture her whipping the rookies as they groveled at her feet. "Fill out zee ficken papers!"

Personally, I had always believed that women should give up bangs after a certain age. Bangs on an older woman made me wonder what major imperfection she was hiding. The bangs and the ponytail together made it hard to take Anna Keller seriously, but then, I could easily imagine her with that whip. I tried being nice to this chick, but made no headway at all. My best defense has always been a good offense. I thought she might be someone I should have as an ally—or at least not have as an enemy—so I tried to break through.

"Anna, my name is Ginger Rogers," I said. "It's a pleasure to meet you."

I think she hissed at me. She looked me up and down, then said, "I give you three weeks, tops."

Bitch. I don't give up easily, however. "I work directly for the Bott," I said.

Frau Keller turned so quickly that it startled me into silence. "There are no brokers that work directly for the Bott. That does not exist *You* do not exist."

Apparently, I really was scum after all.

—∞∞—

Like any group of rookies who start something unfamiliar and challenging together, the group of us who started that same day learned to stick together. We really had no clue what was happening at Stratton Oakmont, and what would happen to each one of us. We didn't know which of us would end up in the front of the room, and who would fail to make the grade—that is, fail to pass the Series 7. We all sat together in that pathetic break room and hunched over our paperwork as though we were filling out the exam itself.

In fact, we were filling out the Uniform Application for Securities Industry Registration, or U4. The U4 is the industry's registration form for representatives of broker-dealer firms and investment advisers, more commonly known as stockbrokers. The completed form—some forty-odd pages in all—would register me in the appropriate jurisdictions and also linked my name to the U4 electronically in the Central Registration Depository. Registrants had to provide all the information requested, answer all questions, and possibly provide documents to clarify or support their responses. It was their obligation to amend and update information on the Form U4 as changes occurred.

That meant nothing to me at the time. All forms seemed to say something similar, like "Please answer all questions as completely and truthfully as possible." It was no big deal, and I didn't see it as in any way signing my life away or taking on any undue responsibility. It was just a piece of paper that would allow sweet Ginger Rogers the right to get rich by making money for other people. Selling was selling, right? And how hard could it be? Buy low, sell high, right? Or was it buy high, sell low…? It didn't matter; they were going to train me, so I didn't have to know anything. And as long as I filled out the form correctly to the best of my ability, I figured all I had to do was soak up the information, pass that damn test, and then wait for the money to start rolling in. Oh, and *pick up the fuckin' phone*, as Frankie had told us.

The U4 forms were retained by the filing firm, which in my case was Stratton Oakmont. The information in them had to be accurate and up to date, and it could all be disclosed publicly upon request, including our social security numbers, full names, addresses, and dates of birth. The securities industry was a world of its own. I couldn't tell if the fact that the information of individual brokers could be laid bare to the world suggested an assumption of innocence or an assumption of guilt.

The paperwork we would return to Frau Keller before nine o'clock would set the wheels in motion for the rookies to become sucked into the Stratton Oakmont process. Our training would begin soon for us to prepare for the Series 7 exam, and as John told us, the test was a bitch but if we were good test takers, we'd do fine. I was an exceptional test taker, so I was not worried that I was a clothing designer, not a rocket scientist. Besides, how many rocket scientists could pass the Series 7? I pondered the amusing thought that a dummy like me could easily become a broker in several months. A money-strapped fashionista who half the time lost track of her own checkbook was about to be entrusted with other people's money.

I studied the form. "Provide general information," it said. I did not find it very general. It looked more as though they wanted a detailed description of my entire life.

Did I have a professional designation? *What was that, a street name, or a stage name? Did Sweet Ginger apply?*

Had I ever changed my name? *Well, yes, I'd been married twice and I had taken Antonio's last name, and then Freddy's last name.*

What other names or nicknames, (or aliases?) had I been known by? *Should I add "scum of the earth cold caller" to the list?*

Where had I lived? *Long Island, Manhattan, Long Island, Manhattan, Long Island...*

Where had I been employed? *Did I have to include the six weeks I worked at the jewelry kiosk at the mall the summer I was sixteen?*

Did I have any relevant business disclosures? *Hmmm, should I mention that every Garment Center business I ever worked for except The Right Bank had gone out of business?*

Did I have any criminal disclosures? *My late husband had been shot during a drug deal gone bad, and although I personally indulged in the use of certain illegal substances on occasion as well, I had never been arrested. And it wasn't as though I was an ax murderer, right?*

The form also included a number of sections for brokers who were already licensed, including regulatory action disclosure; civil judicial disclosure; customer complaint/arbitration/civil litigation disclosure; and termination disclosure. I skipped right over all that, barely giving it a thought. After all, that would never apply to me. I was not yet licensed and had no understanding of what that meant or how it related to me...

I handed over my completed paperwork to Anna Keller and showed her two forms of photo ID, which she photocopied and hand-transcribed onto a form. Then she introduced me to Amy, a trainee who had been with the firm for a little over two months. I cannot imagine why Frau Keller thought Amy and I would make a good pair; aside from gender, we had nothing in common. Amy was half my age, and a baby-faced, perky blond bimbo, what was known as a Long Island Valley Girl. Like the eponymous California version, Long Island Valley Girls were white "Material Girls," all about superficial considerations and looking the part rather than actually pursuing any kind of personal development. But along with the rising intonation that made everything sound like a question ("Like, my name is Amy?"), they spoke with the unique Lawn Guyland accent.

I love clothes, of course, and always cared a lot about my looks and appearance. But I had also worked hard to neutralize my tendency to sound like Mike Myers doing Linda Richman doing the *cawfee tawk* routine. It was hard enough getting some people to deal with a woman on the phone, so I had made serious effort to scrape away any inflection or slang that made me sound like a ditz. I had to admit, though, that Amy's singsong falsetto was rather pleasant as background music, and she could be adorable (like, *totally*). And while working at Stratton Oakmont was probably a fairly decent paying job for her, it was obvious that she was less interested in becoming a stockbroker than in becoming a stockbroker's wife. Since she was not a very bright girl, her plan to date and marry a rich broker was the closest she'd ever come to a solid career plan. She would find a lot to work with at Stratton Oakmont, where there were dozens of single, decent-looking men: fat men, thin men, old men, and young men. We were surrounded by available men. And to think that I had spent ten years of my life going to singles bars, and using dating services! I could have just worked at Stratton Oakmont. The place was packed with men who had money and readily spent it, especially if they thought that it increased their chances that they might get laid.

I did strike up a few friendships with a couple of the rookies. I found most of them fairly easy to relate to, even though they were so incredibly different from any of my other friends. My first broker buddy was Sal Angelli, another Tony-style Guido in both looks and attire. Sal was an amazingly smooth talker, with the charm and ease of a con artist, and certainly did not fit anyone's description of an investment banker.

"Sal? I'm Ginger Rogers," I said, when Amy introduced us. "Nice to meet you."

"Ginger Rogers? Can I have this dance? Just kidding. I'm sure that you get that a lot!"

"No, not really. You're the first person that has ever said that!" I said, dead-pan. "Why?" I looked at Sal's face until I could tell he thought I was serious, then I cracked a smile. "Hey, I'm kidding!"

Sal heaved a sigh of relief. Sal was about my age, of average height and thin, with beautiful blue eyes that reminded me of Antonio's, which may be part of why I liked him. He wore his hair in a dated center part, a look more popular among young men in the '60s than the '90s. Another reason he stood out was his habit of accessorizing his expensive suits with cowboy boots and the most garish ties on Wall Street.

"So, what brings you to Stratton Oakmont?" he asked me.

"I want to make a boatload of money. This seems to be a good place to do that. You?"

"After selling my limousine company, I needed something else to do. So I answered an ad in *Newsday*."

Sal was working for a newly licensed broker, Sam Levy, who did not have the power or experience that the Bott had. I could tell that Sal would be great as a broker; he seemed born to it. He was often driven to work in a limousine, one of the perks of having sold his company. Sal seemed brighter than the typical broker at Stratton Oakmont, in a street-smart way. It was Sal who would eventually sit me down and tell me the facts of life at Stratton Oakmont. He was the one that explained to me that at Stratton Oakmont, it was all about liquidity. He was one of the first in our group to figure it out.

The other rookie I befriended early on was Mike Rosen. Mike and I became fast friends.

"Hi, I'm Ginger Rogers."

"Mike Rosen. Nice to meet you, Ginger. And what brings you to Stratton Oakmont?"

"Money." That said it all.

He nodded. "Yeah, I hear that. I worked for an electronics store for many years. I always thought that one day I would own it. But we just couldn't compete with the superstores—the Wal-Marts, the Best Buys, even the Crazy Eddies. We couldn't even come close to their prices." He said. "I got married five years ago, and I have two very young daughters to support. So here I am, though I'm not really sure that this is right for me. My wife's cousin, Randy Cohen, brought me in, and said he'd take me under his wing, teach me everything he knows. I'm worried because I'm such a slow learner."

"You'll be fine. I can tell." He seemed very intelligent to me. I hoped that I would be fine, too. I didn't have a mentor on the inside.

Mike, Sal, and I were all married with children. We had all jumped into the same lifeboat after midlife career changes. "What about you, Ginger?" he asked me. "Married? Divorced? Kids?"

"Yes, no, and yes," I answered. No need to mention Antonio. That was a painful subject and I rarely brought it up. "I'm married to a Puerto Rican guy with two children, two boys. We live in a tiny house in Port Washington."

My mind raced back to when we bought the house. I will never forget that closing. I had not believed my darling Freddy, who loved to play practical jokes, when he told me that the bank had called my former boss and discovered that I was no longer working there. Why would they do that? And why would Lenny tell them that I no longer worked there? Well, it was true, but still…I had been fired when Lenny decided to file for bankruptcy again.

"Hey, Len, it's Ginger. What's goin' on? I heard you told the bank that I don't work for you anymore," I said. "Lenny, this is going to cost me the house—you know that, don't you?" I was pretty upset, but I kept my cool.

"Ginger, *Dahling*, you know I love you," he said. "But you're asking me to *lie* for you." I wanted to scream. The man bullshitted everyone about everything. Why would he have a problem lying to the bank? "Hold on, Ginger, the bank is actually calling me right now on the other line."

"Lenny, please!"

It seemed like hours had passed, but it was actually less than a minute before Lenny was back on the line. "I bought you some time. I told them that I had no clue what was going on, that I was only renting space here. They asked for written documentation that you are working for Madisons. Sorry, Ginger." He hung up. I couldn't believe it. What could I do?

I called Neil Hautz. He would know what to do. Technically he was still a big boss over there.

"Neil, hey, it's Ginger," I said. "What's goin' on?"

"Hey, Ginger! Great to hear you voice! Did you close on your house yet?"

"Funny you should ask…" I said. I told Neil that the bank was balking because I no longer worked for Madisons, and asked if there was any way he could fax something to the bank that would save me. Neil was a good friend, but he wasn't a fool; he wouldn't put anything on paper without talking to his lawyer, but he told me to sit tight for an hour or so while he thought things through.

Finally, he called me back. "I just spoke to the bank," he said. "You're fine, and you owe me."

"Did you fax over a statement?"

"No. I told the woman that I was really sorry for not calling back until now, and could she believe that the hotel that I'm staying at here in El Salvador just gave me the message?" he said, chuckling. "Worse, this godforsaken hovel barely has running water, let alone a fax machine. Of course the woman who wants to buy the house works for me. She is out on vacation." Vague, impossible to verify, believable. I loved it. And just like that, the closing was on!

I told Mike how I had been so nervous at the closing that I could barely talk. I kept waiting for someone to burst into the room and shout, "Stop the closing! This woman is a fraud!" And maybe I was, but I *had* worked there… and I shouldn't have been fired…and I really, really, really wanted that house.

Mike, like me, desperately needed to make money for his children. He was the main breadwinner for the family—his wife only worked part-time—but I thought he was luckier than most of the pathetic bunch of trainees surrounding me in that he had a mentor. Randy Cohen was one of the largest (literally and figuratively) brokers at Stratton. He was so ripped that his arms could never hang straight down next to his body, it was as though he had toothpicks in his armpits. On our first day there, Randy charged over to Mike and spoke loudly in Brooklyn gangsterese. "Hey, dis kid? He's wit me. You take cayah of my boy—make sure nuttin' bad goes down. Anyting he needs, you give 'im, or you ansuh to me, capiche?"

Mike played it really cool, staring down at his loafers. I guess he knew the type of guy he was dealing with; after that first day, I never saw Randy in the back of the room again. Furthermore, Randy never said more than two words to Mike after that. Like us, Mike was on his own. So much for having a mentor.

At eleven thirty, the new recruits were assembled once more in the break room. John told us that we were going to hear from another one of the Stratton Oakmont principals, Josh Shamus, who was a recovering alcoholic—and a recovering garmento. He appeared to be around forty, no more than 5'5, and average looking. A vain man would have said he had a receding hairline, but Josh would have been bluntly honest and said he was balding. He seemed at ease with painting himself in a less than flattering light. He seemed friendly and approachable, unlike Frankie Porter.

Josh grabbed a cup of black coffee and stood before us, holding it in both hands in front of his face and blowing across the top of the drip-stained mug. "Before coming to Stratton Oakmont, I worked as a dress salesman in the Garment Center," he said. He took a sip, found it still too hot, and set it down on the counter. "I was such a failure as a salesman that I could not hold a job. Not surprisingly, I developed a big problem with alcohol." Somehow, it was easy to picture him dead drunk, rolling around in the gutter. "I spent five years of my life working for seven different companies, all in 1407. I left the Garment Center three years ago, and now I make a million dollars a year at Stratton Oakmont."

No way!

"My entire family was against this change," he said. "They told me I would never pass the test. I passed it. They told me that I was wasting my time. I didn't think so. They told me I was not a good salesman. I thought I just sucked at selling clothes."

We all laughed. He was a good speaker. And he gave us hope.

"They told me that I should stick to the rag trade, to stick with what I knew. Even though I was failing at it and it was making me miserable, it was safe." He paused, and drank down the whole mug of coffee in one long gulp. "Thank god I didn't listen to them."

He laughed. He was just getting warmed up. "Several months ago, I bought a house for my dad, the one person who has always been there for me. I paid cash. That's what this business is all about. We take care of family."

"You have an unbelievable opportunity here at Stratton Oakmont to make money for yourself. More importantly, you have the chance to make money for your family. Maybe you've been at the bottom, too. Maybe that's why you're here. I want you all to stand up and introduce yourselves, one by one, and tell me what you want to do for your family."

Josh gave an extremely emotional and touching speech. I'd never been to an AA meeting, but I had a pretty good idea after that talk what it was like. Every time he told us about another low point in his life, another bad decision he'd made, he made us feel like he could see into our hearts, like he knew how much we wanted to climb out of our financial gutters and earn some real money. Of course, what he didn't tell us was that what he was doing was *all* he did for Stratton Oakmont. He never mentioned that he *still* couldn't sell shit. He never mentioned that if he hadn't been best friends and golf buddies with Frankie, he would probably would have gotten the boot from Stratton Oakmont just as he had from every other place he'd ever worked.

Looking back, though, I know it wouldn't have mattered if he'd told us. I was hooked.

I learned a lot that day, including the fact that the bigwigs at Stratton Oakmont considered themselves some sort of Jewish mafia, or as we called them, the Kosher Nostra. They were all completely obsessed with and constantly making references to the mob, to the importance of being loyal to the family. The two words came up again and again that first day: loyalty and family. I would not have been surprised to find that if one of us were to threaten to leave, we would wake up the next day with a horse's head in our bed.

None of us seemed inclined to quit after that first day, although I could tell that there were a couple in my group who would probably wash out. Very few people are cut out for cold calling, but I knew that I was one of them. The years that I had spent working in the Garment Center had made me into exactly the kind of hard-ass the job demanded. We used to swap stories about buyers who would look us straight in the eye and ask for markdown money, even though they knew and we knew that they had sold our garments at full price. And we'd have no choice but to fork the shakedown money over, because if we refused to pay them, we would never get our lines into that particular store again. I recalled the day that I shared a cab with Michael, the owner of the sportswear company that I worked for at the time. He showed me a wad of cash—ten thousand dollars in big bills—he was carrying to pay off a notorious buyer who wouldn't even consider looking at a line without money up front. *Cash money*, they called it in the hood—and in the Garment Center. You had to be hard-nosed in soft goods.

4

REBUTTALS

THERE WAS NO doubt in my mind that cold calling would be a piece of cake.

The first week of work was strictly a listen-and-learn training experience. We were told to grab chairs and listen to some of the more experienced guys in the cold-calling section. That was the wildest section of the trainee half of the room. It consisted of rows and rows of desks, one on top of the other, so that callers usually had to shout into the phones to be heard over other people shouting into phones. Cold callers were told to think on their feet, so most of the good ones never used a chair. *Never sit down! Get excited! Excitement sells!*

I could tell I would be one of the callers who paced back and forth when pitching. I couldn't wait. The other thing I couldn't wait for was to get my name on the whiteboard. The one in the front of the room was for brokers, but the one in the back was for trainees who got leads. The first week I noticed that it only had one or two names on it at any given time. John told us that we would be entitled to write our names on the board as soon as we got ten leads. I had no idea how hard it was to get ten leads, but neither did anyone else. Given my extremely competitive nature, I was certain of one thing, I *had* to be the first of our group to get my name on that board, and as soon as possible.

My workday at Stratton Oakmont was extremely regimented, almost like boot camp. We had to report to work by seven thirty. Latecomers risked not finding a desk, and since there were more trainees than desks, those who missed out were sent home for the day, which meant a day's docked pay. From seven thirty to eight we had skill-mills, when the Bott and John helped us work on our rebuttals. The Bott would shout an objection, then point a sausagelike finger at someone in the trainee group and demand a reply. God help anyone who didn't know the proper response. The Bott would rip that unfortunate soul a new one, publicly, loudly, and without apology. It was awful. The Bott was slightly more gentle with the ten newbies, so I was typically spared complete humiliation in front of a hundred or so other cold callers. For me, it was not knowing the proper rebuttal that frightened me but the idea of *pitching the room*, as they called it. Public speaking in front of large groups has never been my thing. On the other hand, get me on the phone one-on-one with a total stranger and I was a tigress.

We'd been given a long script of typical objections and the rebuttals we should learn:

OBJECTION: "I'm not interested."

REBUTTAL: "I didn't *expect* you to be interested in a thirty-second conversation. Take a look at my information you *will* be impressed!"

OBJECTION: "I have no money."

REBUTTAL: "Save that for the other ten guys that call you. If I thought for a minute that you had no money, I would not be talking to you."

OBJECTION: "My wife is a broker."

REBUTTAL: "My husband has a wife who is a broker, and he deals with other people!"

It was crucial to study and practice the rebuttals. Stammering and stuttering on a phone call would not make us rich. Every night on my drive home, I practiced saying anything that I had tripped over during the day. The hardest for me, for some reason, was the company name. While I drove I would say it out loud, over and over: *Stratton Oakmont, Stratton Oakmont, Stratton Oakmont.* It had to be smooth, which wasn't easy with all those hard consonants and Germanic sounds.

At eight, we started making calls, before the secretaries—the gatekeepers—got in. The rule of thumb seemed to be that the nicer the executive, the nastier the gatekeeper. One of the more experienced brokers, Tommy Renninger, told me about an experience he'd had cold-calling a prospect with a very tough gatekeeper.

Tommy had a very deep, commanding voice, and he used it to great effect. "Bob Jones, please. This is Tommy Renniger from Stratton Oakmont. Thank you."

He kept his words short and all business. Such authoritative and self-assured directives unnerved the tough ones, since all the other callers gave the gatekeepers a chance to reject them. They would ask, "Is Bob Jones there?"

Typically, the gatekeeper would respond with, "Who's calling?" But in that case, Tommy had already said who was calling. He'd already answered the follow-up question of the name of his company.

According to Tommy, the last two words were the most important: "When you say 'Thank you,' you're essentially saying 'Dismissed!'" he said. "You're saying, 'Get Bob Jones on the phone now and stop wasting my time.'"

It worked.

All I had to do was follow the program. As Frankie told us often enough, we had to work smarter, not harder. *Just pick up the fuckin' phone.* My personal goal was to turn four hundred calls a day into thirty contacts and ten qualified leads. We took a break from calling for the general meeting for trainees, which was held between nine and nine thirty, and made calls until lunchtime.

Officially, lunch was from noon to one. Unofficially, we were discouraged from taking lunch or at least from leaving the building. That reminded me of a broker I had dated once who had confided that the last time he had gone out to lunch on a workday had been the day President Kennedy had been shot. He'd returned to his desk to find that all hell had broken out, and when he finally checked out his stocks it was too late. He never left his office at lunch again. I decided to follow his lead and eat at my desk.

We made calls all afternoon until four, when the market closed, at which point we had another general meeting for the entire boardroom. The meeting was generally followed by some kind of training session, and it was usually seven o'clock by the time I left the office.

At home I found it increasingly difficult to turn off the aggressive salesperson I was at work. At Stratton Oakmont, I was not just another woman, I was a force to be reckoned with! The hot, sweet Ginger that Freddy loved was still in there somewhere, but more often than not the person who walked in the door at first was bad-ass Ginger Rogers from Stratton fuckin' Oakmont. My poor Freddy! Where was the sweet woman he had married? Where was the nurturing mother to our two lovely kids?

Likewise, I had to turn into that bad-ass woman before I walked into work. Before I was allowed to get on the phone, I had to memorize the pitch. Qualifying someone as a lead meant asking clients about the size of their port-folios, learning the names of several stocks that they already owned, finding out the names of their current brokers, and finding out the last time they had traded. Qualified prospects had to have a minimum portfolio of $100,000, had to buy NASDAQ stocks (which were considered more speculative), and had to have bought stock within the last year. I'll never forget the pitch.

"Mr. Jones? Ginger Rogers from Stratton Oakmont. How are you today?" I'd wait for a response, but cut things off if it went on too long. "Great! Have you heard of my firm, Stratton Oakmont? Does the name ring a bell?" Again, I'd often push right past any response. "I represent one of the leading NASDAQ underwriters in the country. What I'd like to do today is send you a copy of my track record and, more importantly, down the road get back to you and share an idea. Fair enough?"

Anybody who did not agree at that point was not a lead. In that case, I would end the phone call quickly. For those who did answer positively, I'd verify the mailing address, which had the dual purpose of making sure the person was not trying to fake me out, and also showed the prospect that I knew something about the person with whom I was speaking and was therefore not some fly-by-night scam artist. "Is your best address, 1234 Whatever Lane? Great. And just so I don't waste your time in the future, do you have any preference for Big Board or OTC? Perfect. Can you tell me the names of two stocks that you currently own?"

Anybody who would not tell me the names of two stocks already owned was not a lead. Otherwise, I pressed on. "Which broker do you work with?" Again, anyone who would give the broker's name was not a lead.

Then came the final question, which most prospects—if they answered at all—would lie about. "One last thing, and I'll get you right off the phone. Ballpark, what are you working with in the market?" The goal was to end up with a dollar amount, although it was probably not a real number. "Great.

Thank you for your time. Once again, my name is Ginger Rogers, the company is Stratton Oakmont," I say smoothly. "I'll get this information right out to you. All I ask is that in the future, when I get back to you, I get five minutes and an open ear. Okay?"

It was a simple word, that "okay" tacked on the end, but it was the most important part of the pitch. Anyone who did not say "okay" was not receptive, and really not a lead.

I learned a lot during those first few weeks. Cold calling was strictly a numbers game. If I made four hundred calls a day, and I was prospecting every day, I should get ten leads every day if my pitch sounded halfway decent. Ten new leads would generally translate into three new accounts. New accounts meant a commission for me. Of course, it wouldn't be easy to make four hundred calls in a single day, but it could be done. I would just need to tune out the entire room, and focus. I found that, as a woman, I had a much higher success rate at getting past the gatekeepers. My deep, throaty voice made many of the gatekeepers reluctant to ask questions. As far as I was concerned, in sales it was completely acceptable to flirt my ass off with a prospect to get a lead, and if that meant hinting somehow to the gatekeeper that my call might be personal rather than professional, I was fine with that. One thing I could count on was that most male C-level executives loved to tell me how great they were. If I rolled with that, I would generally get the lead.

When she found out what I was doing, my friend Pam had the best advice. "You have to understand that all wealthy men have girlfriends, and their secretaries usually know this," Pam said. "Before I ask for someone, the first thing I do is imagine that I've just given the guy the best blow job of his life. Then I make up a pet name for him. For example, if his name is Richard, I'll say to the secretary, in a seductive voice, 'Is Dickey in?'"

What happens?

The secretaries are usually too embarrassed to ask anything at all, and I get right through. If they do ask something, it's typically something like, "Ddd-does he know you?" and when I say, Oh, I think you could say that... they put me through.

I always responded to the gatekeepers' questions and added one of my own. It confused them, as they were often so entrenched in their routine that they didn't know what to do when someone strayed from the expected script.

"Bobby Jones, please."

"Who's calling?"

"Ginger Rogers from Stratton Oakmont. Is he in?"

"Ohhhh. Well, where are you from?"

When that happened, I would get a little annoyed. I had already told her where I was from! So I would repeat myself slowly and take my cue from Tommy Renniger's strategy. "Ginger Rogers from Stratton Oakmont. Can you connect me to Bobby? Thank you." I couldn't say "thank you" with the *exact* tone Tommy would use: many old-school gatekeepers would accept a dismissive tone from a man and think he was assertive, but hear the exact same tone from a woman and think she was a bitch.

"Does he know you?"

"I certainly hope so," I would counter. "Is he in?"

"Does he know what this is about?"

"I certainly hope so. Is he in?" The key factor was to never lie.

"What's this in reference to?"

"It is in reference to Stratton Oakmont. He's familiar. I can hold. Thank you." I would use a tone that was professional and as free as possible of any edge that would make the gatekeeper think *bitch!*, but also something firm enough to convey that I meant business. Something that said, "Stop asking so many fuckin' questions and get him on the fuckin' phone!"

After a week of training, I was starting to get good. Between working in the Garment Center and spending ten years doing the dating scene, I was an unbelievable schmoozer. All those blind dates were finally paying off. I had always found it very easy to get into conversations with total strangers. That was a bonus. Although I knew nothing about the stock market, I was educated, well traveled, and a great bull-shitter. I could improvise, unlike those telemarketers who got lost if they were somehow taken off their script. The fourth day on the phone, I was calling Dun & Bradstreet leads. Good old D & Bs were the hardest to cold call because *everyone* used D & B as a lead source, so prospects were inundated with calls from salespeople in all kinds of different industries. The calls were hard, but that first day I got seven leads, and became a star. The Bott decided that my name should be changed to Killer. Every broker in the room promised me that I would be rich soon. I was thrilled! I knew that I was on my way.

The first time I got ten leads I was so excited I could barely hold the pen as I wrote my name on the board. I was shocked to find that most of the other cold callers were not very happy for me. Many were actually pissed off.

"You got ten leads?" they said, challenging me as though I would dare lie to the Bott.

I was so happy and pleased with myself that I just laughed. "That's right!"

When my name started to appear on the board on a regular basis, the reactions from the other trainees was often outright hostility, especially from guys who had been working as cold callers at Stratton Oakmont for two, three, or even six months but were only getting three leads a day. They treated me as though I was cheating somehow, but all I was doing was using psychology. I helped my prospects stroke their own egos.

My buddy Mike fell into that category of guys who were struggling. He had told me that he was a slow learner, but I couldn't understand why. He was obviously intelligent, and I could tell that he'd make it if he kept at it, and that he would become the type of broker who would really try to make his clients money.

Sal was quickly becoming as successful as I expected him to be, making ten leads every day. There were only a handful of names on the board every day, so either he was a superstar or he was writing wood—fake leads. Some guys who worked as cold callers either sucked at it or were just lazy, or sucked at it *because* they were lazy.

Amy, the cute blond bimbo that I started with actually did much better than I ever thought possible. I suppose she got the "sympathy" lead. She was so pathetic on the phone that prospects probably felt sorry for her. It didn't matter, though. She'd never pass the Series 7, and there was no way that she would make it as a broker even if by some miracle she did pass the exam. She was so busy working the room, schmoozing with the single men, that she was rarely on the phone anyway. I wondered why the Bott put up with her.

I got my answer soon enough, when one evening the Bott scheduled a five o'clock training with his newest cold callers. I was beginning to understand the pecking order that existed within Stratton Oakmont. Although the Bott was up toward the top, he did not seem to be part of the inner circle of buddies that met behind closed doors every day. There were multiple owners of Stratton Oakmont, but only three who went to the office and ran the show: Frankie,

Josh, and Glen. They were all former garmentos from Bayside. The Bott was a former garmento, too, but he was not from Bayside.

Bayside, located in northeastern Queens, is a suburban neighborhood that bordered Long Island. It had city amenities and taxes that were several thousand dollars a year less than Nassau County taxes—despite being almost right next door. Bayside's crowded main street makes it seem like a mini-Manhattan. One block over the wide, tree-lined streets complement the fairly pricey homes.

Bayside was the first location that groups of one ethic background or another moved to when their beloved Brooklyn or Bronx started going south. It is just thirty minutes by rail from Manhattan on the Long Island Rail Road. Although historically considered a safe and wealthy neighborhood, Bayside ironically became infamous for more than one violent clash related to organized crime, including one that took place shortly before I started working at Stratton Oakmont. Bayside resident and reputed mobster Michael Pappadio worked for the Lucchese crime family, although as far as his wife knew he merely managed the Lucchese family's interests in the Garment Center. Pappadio fell out of favor with the Luccheses, and was instructed to leave the garment business behind. When he refused, he was ambushed in a Brooklyn bagel shop, called the Crown Bagel, by two mobsters who beat him with a coil of cable, then shot him in the head with a .22-caliber pistol.

The Bott was from Bay Ridge, in Brooklyn, the place where *Saturday Night Fever* had been filmed. That was worlds apart from *The Godfather*, and Stratton Oakmont's beloved family. But even though the Bott was not part of the inner sanctum, he *was* a very successful broker with a large staff. Amy and I were both on his team, and thus attendance at the five o'clock training was mandatory for us. We were joined by several other cold callers who also worked for the Bott, and with scripts in hand we made our way to the conference room.

The evening's training was going to be given by Dave, one of Bott's Boys, as they were often called. I liked Dave. He was an excellent cold caller, and knew how to give a gatekeeper the impression that he was a close friend of Mr. Jones simply by the way he asked for him. I had already learned a lot from Dave.

Dave entered the room with about a dozen cold calling bibles. This was to become second nature to everyone that made the cut.

COLD CALLING BIBLE

ATTITUDE

A) The Right Attitude: To be mentally prepared for challenges which each day may bring.

B) The Right Attitude: to be self-confident, in both a physical and emotional sense to develop the internal fortitude necessary for boredom you to keep on keeping on.

C) The Right Attitude: knowing that you are in the right place at the right time.

Attitude is the single most important element to build on. Without it, there is nothing.

APPROACH

Before we use the "approach" we must understand it. Essentially this is "home plate"-no moves can occur until you get out of the so-called "batter's box."

The ingredients of a successful "approach are simple:

1. Good telephone voice
2. Precise Punctuation.
3. Quality
4. Brevity
5. Excitement with a lean towards accuracy rather than boredom.

With these simple ingredients the game can start.

Basic telephone Approach (tailored to your personality)

DAILY SCHEDULE
7:30-7:45 BREAKFAST- WALL STREET JOURNAL- REPORT
7:45-8:00 WARM-UP-START COLD CALLING
8:00-8:15 SKILL MILLS
8:15-8:30 BOARDROOM MEETING

8:30-9:00 TRAINEE MEETING
9:00 -12:30 COLD CALL
12:30-1:00 LUNCH
1:00-4:45 COLD CALL
4:45-5:00 TRAINEE MEETING
5:00-5:30 BOARDROOM MEETING
AVERAGE TOTAL HOURS PER DAY=8 HOURS FOR PROSPECTING GOAL-50 ATTEMPTS PER HOUR-50 CONTACTS PER DAY: 7-10 QUALIFIED INVESTORS.

COLD CALLING BIBLE

QUALIFYING CALL

"Hello, Mr. (first and last name) please! Mr. (last name) (RR name) fom Stratton Oakmont in NY. How are you today?"

"Great"

"Sir, I know you're busy, I'll get right to the point."

"Are you familiar with (the name, firm) Stratton Oakmont?"

(if yes) " Do you presently have an account with Stratton Oakmont?"

(if no) "That's fine, you may not be. We specialize in both foreign and domestic special situations, new issues, secondaries… things of that nature."

"Very simply sir, with your permission, all I would like to do is introduce myself and my firm, forward you a complimentary issue of our monthly research report and down the road get back to you with our next recommendation"

"Fair enough?"

(If yes) "Just a few quick questions so in the future I never waste your time.

(If no) Don't waste time with unqualified prospects.

"Are you presently invested in the market?"

"From what I understand you're invested in the past?"(He may not have done something in a while).

"From what I understand you deal with a local broker?"

REBUTALS:
Remember your time is valuable, do not wasted with prospects that are not qualified.

NOT INTERESTED:
Q: Are you presently in the market?'(If yes clarify that):
"We only make a handful of recommendation a year"
(If no, maybe hasn't done something recently) "From what I understand you're invested in the past
      Or
"From what I understand, you invest with a local broker?"

OTHER BROKER
LOCAL BROKER: "That's great we are not looking to interfere with any-thing you're currently doing. "I was only hoping that down the road, when we isolate a situation with strong potential to make you money, you would have an open ear." Fair enough?"

"Believe me we wouldn't be calling you if you didn't. Most of our clients have 2 or 3." "Stratton is a boutique investment banking firm making only a handful of recommendations a year, and I was only hoping that one time down the road, run an idea by you,
      -if you like it perhaps we could do business.
      -if not you will never hear from me again.
"What do you say.?"

REBUTTALS

ALOT OF THESE CALLS:

"I'm sure you get bombarded with these calls."

I'm sure (hope) you can tell the good from the bad."

Stratton Oakmont is a boutique investment bank making only a handful of recommendations a year." At this point I am only hoping to introduce myself and my firm and get back to you with the next major recommendation." Fair enough?"

I am NOT trying to sell you anything, I don't even have a stock to recommend." I'm simply asking for your permission to properly introduce myself, send you my card and some basic information on my firm, and one time, down the road share an idea with you." Fair enough/"

Mr. _____, you should be very happy about that, you're a successful businessman." It's when you stop getting them you should start to worry."

HAPPY WITH BROKER

"That's great." Believe me I'm not looking to run your portfolio." "Stratton Oakmont is a boutique investment banking firm making only a handful of recommendations a year." "I am only asking for that one time when I see an idea that can make you money you would have an open ear." "Fair enough?"

"I didn't think otherwise, however, I'm sure you'll agree that no one person or one firm for that matter has a monopoly on ideas." Stratton Oakmont is a boutique investment banking firm specializing in distress and undervalued blue chips new issues, secondaries…. things of that nature.

COLD CALLING BIBLE

REAL ESTATE:

"Great investment but you don't have the liquidity or the diversification of the market?" In this type of (investment economic environment) you should make a move without that."

BROTHER/FRIEND/COUSIN

"Don't let your personal relationships interfere with your ability to make money in the market." "Stratton open on makes only a handful of recommendations for a year, so you won't be hearing from me too often." Very simply, when we're moving on our next investment opportunity, I'd like to be able to call you and run it by you."

COLD CALLING BIBLE

QUALIFYING QUESTIONS

"So, I'd never waste your time with an inappropriate investment what's something that was not suitable to you."

Do you prefer big keyboard or over the counter (OTC)?"

"Have you invest in internationally? Japan Mexico Germany?"

"When you invest do you usually invest more long term or more short term?"

And by nature, are you more aggressive or more conservative?"

Nothing specific, approximately how much do you have in the market?" Ballpark figure."

"When you like and I idea, what's a comparable dollar range you normally work with? "Ballpark?" (If the answer is "I don't know ")

"If I came back to you with an idea that you like, and the timing is right - ballpark what would you feel comfortable with? "Ballpark." Great."

"So I know (what you like) or (your investment objectives), can you name me a few stocks that you recently purchased or are currently holding?"

"Mr. _____, what I'll do is have my secretary forward that out." If you have any questions please feel free to give me a call."

"Thanks for your time."

WHAT IS A QUALIFIED INVESTOR?

1) Any corporation or individual investor with 100K or more in the stock market.
2) Any investor with 100K or more in the stock market that is somewhat receptive. I say somewhat because they don't have to be overjoyed that they heard from you.

FOR A BETTER QUALIFIED LEAD THE FOLLOWING INFORMATION WOULD BENEFIT BOTH THE BROKER AND THE PROSPECT:

1) Big Board, OTC or International Investments
2) aggressive or conservative
3) More long term or short term
4) Ballpark number/ amount in the market
5) Comfort level on an idea.
6) Are of interest (eg: drugs, auto, biotech, etc.)
7) Most recent investment.

Do's

1) Be an example of what a broker trainee should be.
2) Separate yourself from the crowd. Eagles don't flock, you find them one at a time.
3) Always be polite and professional. Each contact that you make is a representation of the firm and its image.
4) Try to keep motivated and energetic throughout the day. This will build endurance and be the most important foundation for your success. This business is not a sprint but a marathon. Don't ever forget that.
5) Make the most of your day, keep focused and keep your eyes on your goal.... Daily, weekly, monthly etc.
6) Play by the numbers. It is proven, stick to it. Speak to 50 people a day or 5/6 an hour. This is a contact sport, the more people you contact, the better you will actually do!

7) Thank every prospect (good, bad or indifferent) for their time. It helps keep you out of trouble and people will understand that you are only doing your job. Trying to make a living.

8) Never ever think or believe that you are just a cold caller, no matter what I say or anyone else. You are an apprentice of a stock broker who is learning a career. Simply put. A broker trainee.

9) Be prepared to live for your first two years like no one else. Working harder than you ever thought possible and for the rest of your life you will live like no one can.

COLD CALLING BIBLE

OTHER TIPS

STICK TO THE PROGRAM
LISTEN TO WHAT THE MAN SAYS
BE A GOOD LISTENER
BE COCKY CONFIDENT
FIND A ROLE MODEL OR MENTOR
BE CONSISTENT-NOT FAIR WEATHER

DON'TS

1) Pick up bad habits. You first make your habits, then your habits make you. This is the most important philosophy for you to understand. You don't suddenly have a bad habit.; for example, you don't become an alcoholic or suddenly become a drug addict. You make one mistake then another and another and this creates a bad habit. Once it is a habit it is almost impossible to break. Think about it, we are all creatures of habit. We wake up at the same time, we eat the same things, we go to the same hangouts and say the same things over and over. Don't let destructive behavior become a habit.

2) Never ever be discourteous to a prospect or their secretary. How foolish could one be? You told them .your name and the firm which you represent. This will certainly come back to haunt you, the broker and the firm that you work for. Save yourself the heartache and the embarrassment by keeping your composure. Be polite. apologetic, respectful and professional.

3) Don't waste your time, there are only so many hours in a day, and so many minutes in an hour. Every minute counts- every single minute. You spend most of your dday trying to make contact, you've got to get the dials in/

4) Never comment on or after each phone call or lead. Everyone has a story to tell.either this or that., nobody wants to hear it. Nobody. Just get your leads and do your job, that's it.Who cares how your conversation with Mr. Jones went? Good or bad' who cares?

5) Don't ever waste your time talking and screwing around with other brokers or trainees. At se the end of the day you are judged on your performance, and so is the fool next to you who lets you distract him. You are all on a mission to be a great cold caller, pass your test and be a successful stockbroker. .Any other activity beyond your mission is a waste of time (see # 3 on Wasting time or # 1 on Bad Habits, for a more detailed explanation).

6) Don't make non-productive phone calls either to friends outside or brokers inside the firm.The phones in the boardroom are for business, period.

7) Never drift into space while cold calling. Stay focused and pumped. Keep your blood pumping by standing and moving around.
   WHY
   a) If he's up-your down= no conversation
   b) He's down+ you're down= no conversation
   c) If he's down –you're up= no conversation
   d) He's up+ you're up= conversation is up
   e)

8) Never let forces outside of your immediate control to bring you down
   (a) a lack of money – that will change.
   (b) Delinquent bills - will never change.
   (c) Negative people- dream stopper that will never change.
   (d) A bad day gets you down it's a numbers game.

9) Never over state who you are.

10) Never comment on the market, pass prospects to your RR

11) Don't take too many breaks, 2 per day besides lunch is plenty. More than that is unnecessary

12) Don't think your two or three leads are better than someone else. Who has 7 or 10? It is a numbers game.

13) Never deviate from the program. This has been proven time and time again. It started in the 70's when Marty Shafflorf of Lehman began cold calling high net worth investors, this has been the way for 20 years - calling the same people over and over again,"If it ain't broke don't fix it."

14) Don't think that you know it all. You are here to learn from people who have done it before. Be a student, a good one and respect your teacher. Don't distract, disrupt or rock the boat your will only be thrown overboard.

15) Don't lack self-confidence. Confucius say all things are difficult before they are easy. You can't possibly be a superstar overnight, it takes time, patience and a lot of hard work. You practice, practice and study, study, study and you take your job very seriously.

16) Never write a wooden lead #1- you're not fooling anyone #2 –It is a waste of time, money, and effort on your part, as well as the firms.

Other tips on Wood

A – Just send the information

B – Real Estate only.

C - Mutual funds bonds and CDs only

D -Has a brother who handles everything

E -Financial advisor

F –Any other waste of valuable time!

COLD CALLING BIBLE

POWER BROKER – BUSINESS PLAN – PBCH04BP
VERY IMPORTANT

The individuals you are calling, all the top executives at that company you're calling, and possibly many others. Many times not only are they excellent retail clientele for Stratton Oakmont but they also maybe a good client for corporate finance relationship.

If a prospect says they are interested in raising money for the company, simply asked them to send us a business plan and mention that for the financials would help.

Have them send it to:

Stratton Oakmont Inc.

1979 Marcus Avenue Suite 120

Lake Success New York 11042

COLD CALLING BIBLE

TO ALL BROKERS AND TRAINEES

FROM:

The individuals you are calling, speaking to a may even be dealing with, are the top executives of the company's you are calling and more often than not a top executive a few others. Many times not only are they excellent retail clientele for Stratton Oakmont, but there is also a chance for an investment banking relationship. As a broker, it is very important for the client to understand what we at Stratton Oakmont do. From corporate finance to working hand in hand with management to achieve their goals. The more you know about your client the better you may serve them. If a prospect or client, expresses an interest in raising money, simply asked them to send us a business plan and don't forget to mention that financial would help.

HAVE THEM SEND IT TO:

STRATTON OAKMONT INC

C/C

1979 MARCUS AVE

LAKE SUCCESS NY 11042

PS: OF COURSE IF SOMETHING HAPPENS THERE WILL BE A FEW SHECKLES FOR YOU.

"When you get the gatekeeper on the phone, you have to talk like it is urgent that you speak to Mr. Jones," he told me. "If you can convey that message through the tone of your voice, you will be an amazing cold caller."

Tonight I liked Dave a little less, as he put me on the spot. "Ginger, you've been very successful as a cold caller. Can you show the guys how you ask for Mr. Jones?"

He wanted me to pitch the room? No, I just couldn't do it. I would choke! Nevertheless, I began. "by keeping your composure. When the gatekeeper answers the phone—"

At that moment, the Bott walked into the conference room and held up a hand to halt the training. He motioned to Amy. "Can you come with me, please? Frankie has asked that you meet him for a drink."

And I thought *I* was being put on the spot.

"Uh...okay? Where?" Her face was flushed pink. What could she say?

"The Garden City Hotel," said the Bott.

"In the lobby bar?" she asked, still hopeful.

"No, suite 302."

Amy looked quite beautiful that day. She wore her long blond hair in the Farrah Faucet shag that still flourished on Long Island. She was dressed in a pink linen skirt and a matching pink cotton cardigan, with a lime green belt and matching lime green shoes. It was a perfect accent color, very Lily Pulitzer. Amy's clothes were so simple that it was impossible to fault the way that she dressed, except that the style did nothing to accent her cute, lean figure. Amy was self-conscious about being so skinny, and vowed that she would "go uptown" as soon as she made some money.

The entire group was stunned. We all looked down at our papers, shuffling them in embarrassed silence. Amy looked ready to cry.

"He wants to meet me...where?"

"Suite 302 of the Garden City Hotel," said the Bott impatiently. "Hurry. He's got a car waiting for you downstairs."

"But—"

"Don't worry. I assure you that nothing unseemly will happen...unless of course you want it to," he said, with a wink. "Trust me."

Riiiiiight. Barry Bottsworth was *so* full of shit. He was sending Amy into the lion's den, and he knew and we all knew it. Worst of all, Amy knew it. I thought of that old joke, "How do you say 'fuck you' in Yiddish? It is simple " Trust me."

She leaned over and whispered to me in a panic. "Ginger, what should I do? If I don't go, "I'll lose my job for sure. If I do go…well, I'm afraid," she whimpered.

"My advice to you? Don't go. From what I've heard, the dude likes fast women and he likes to party. You're asking for trouble."

"But the Bott already told Frankie that I'm on my way. There's a car waiting for me downstairs right now," she wailed. "I can't get fired yet. I'm not done looking for…I haven't…I'm not even a broker yet."

"If you're that afraid of losing your job, then go," I said, shaking my head. "But don't let him get you drunk or high. If he offer you pills, don't take them—he's still into 'ludes. Take one and you'll be horny as hell, which is probably exactly what Frankie is hoping for."

I could tell that Amy felt much better after talking to me, and she assured me that she would come up with escape plan on the ride over there. Whether she trusted the Bott or her own common sense and willpower, she was off to meet Frankie Porter. I worried about her, but in truth I was also a little annoyed that I had to sit through another training session while she got to go off and party with the boss.

The words "sexual harassment" never crossed my mind; in the '90s, women were mostly still grateful to be allowed to sit at the big kid table at all. It would be a decade before people started hauling Wall Streeters into court, like the Smith Barney lawsuit over the infamous Boom-Boom Room. At Stratton Oakmont, the men were not the least bit concerned about the possibility of offending some woman, especially a blond bimbo dumb enough to go to a man's hotel room.

The next morning, I cornered Amy in the break room and demanded she tell me what had happened.

"I figured I could have one, maybe two drinks, and then tell him I had to get home to take care of my sick mother," she said, flopping down on one of the metal folding chairs. "He had different plans. By the time I got there, he'd already taken a couple of Quaaludes, that is, 'ludes, and he was sitting on top of the table smoking a joint."

"Classic…" I muttered.

"He kept giving me champagne, and I kept pretending to drink it, dumping it into the plants when he wasn't looking, you know, and he was so wasted he didn't even seem to notice that I wasn't getting drunk."

"Classy. So, other than trying to get you drunk, was he a gentleman?"

My sarcasm went completely over her head. Amy looked at me like I had lost my mind.

"I kissed Frankie Porter."

"You...kissed him? That same Frankie Porter who screams at the brokers every other morning about how they are the laziest losers on the planet?"

"Yes, that Frankie Porter, the jerk who runs Stratton Oakmont. He tried so hard to get me drunk, but I outsmarted him." She flashed a triumphant smile that faded as quickly as it appeared. "But then...then...I think he realized that he wasn't getting anywhere, and he stood up on the table, unzipped his pants, and whipped out his penis. He just stood there, waving it back and forth at me. Then he said, 'Just kiss me. Kiss me right there.'"

"Oh my fuckin' god. What did you do? Wait, you said...oh, you didn't... oh, you *did*!"

"Ginger, I panicked. I didn't know what to do, so I kissed it and started to just run out of the room. But I had to turn back for my purse, and when I did he...he threw two hundred bucks at me like I was a goddamned hooker!"

She was openly weeping at that point, but then she sat op straight in the chair and smiled. I smiled back. Then she started laughing so hard she could barely talk. "Oh. My. God," she gasped out. "His dick is so freakin' *tiny*!"

The longer I worked at Stratton, the more obvious it was that Frankie's drug addiction was becoming a problem. Even though they were no longer the popular pills of choice they had been in the '80s, the man still really liked his 'ludes. Don't get the wrong idea. I popped a pill now and then myself, including the occasional Quaalude, but it was not cool to do so at work. First, they made me too horny to concentrate, and second, they made me slur my words and they slowed me down. I could never get four hundred calls in if I was knocking back sedatives.

The biggest problem with Frankie's drug habit was that we all had to look to Frankie for guidance. One commonality among all the companies where I'd worked was that employees followed the CEO's lead. Shit flows downhill. When your CEO was habitually late for work, for example, eventually it was established that straggling in late was no big deal. If the CEO was a mean SOB, the people around him slowly turned into bastards, too. And when the CEO was known for wandering into work wasted, that became a recipe for bedlam. I found it pretty amazing that brokers lasted there as long as they did.

When he was straight, Frankie was awesome. I never saw a motivational speaker or salesperson better than Frankie Porter at getting a room excited. He could always give somebody a reason to buy stock, and the sense of urgency to do it immediately. Frankie was usually the one who addressed the room in the morning and afternoon at the general meetings. The longer I worked there, the crazier those meetings became. Frankie must have studied brainwashing techniques, because his specialty was pounding us with the same rhetoric every day.

"At Stratton Oakmont, you have the opportunity to get rich. We do the best deals on the street. Ten years from now, if you tell someone that you worked at Stratton Oakmont in the '90s and didn't make any money, your next sentence will be 'Do you want fries with that?' All you need to do is pick up the phone. Pick up the fuckin' phone. It's not easy, but it's simple."

The problem with Frankie as his drug habit began to get worse, was that his rhetoric began to change. You never knew what to expect. His messages at the meetings ran the gamut from wild enthusiasm to outrageous uncontrolled fury, depending on the day that we had. When we raised new money, he was ecstatic. In 1994, there were close to a thousand employees working the boardroom, and about half of them were licensed brokers. But as with every company, there were a few people pulling most of the weight, a huge number of people putting in a just average performance, and a lot of lazy, underperforming slugs who thought it was fine to wait around for new initial public offerings to jump on. When those slackers did what they usually did, which was nothing, Frankie turned into a demon from hell.

It was hard to blame him: I could see from watching the successful brokers that raising money for Stratton Oakmont by pushing new IPOs was simple and effective. No one wanted to miss out on the next big thing, and our best clients were gamblers at heart. That was how most of the top brokers there raised money. It was easy to do. So, yeah, it did look like Frankie was right, and that most of the brokers were just plain lazy.

What I didn't know yet was that some of them deliberately held back because their clients hated them. And why wouldn't they? They were losing huge sums of money most of the time. When every stock that you're supposed to recommend is down in a bull market, it takes some serious balls to call your customers and tell them to buy more.

"Just pick up the phone," Frankie told us over and over. "Don't try to analyze a stock. Stocks trade. That's what they do. Everyone loves to chase a stock. The time to buy it is now! Mr. Customer, if you liked the company at seven bucks a share, you gotta *love* it at three!"

And because he was the charismatic—if visibly troubled—CEO, the brokers came through for Frankie and raised new money when there was an opportunity to invest in an IPO. And because they delivered when he demanded it, I couldn't understand why they waited for him to demand it. I was too new to understand why they waited for an IPO. Stratton Oakmont had the reputation of doing deals that doubled or tripled the first day! If you were one of the privileged few that were allowed to sell on the first day, you made money.

At the next cold-calling training session, I looked at the group of rookies I had started with. There had been ten of us in the beginning: seven men and three women. Now there were six men and two women—Amy and me. The third woman had been Nicole. To me her pitch sounded smooth and self-assured, very impressive, so I was surprised when she quit. Apparently, she had learned that her little-girl innocence didn't translate over the phone; no one wanted to talk about large sums of money with someone who sounded like a twelve-year-old.

The Bott joined our meeting that morning to evaluate our progress. John was leading the training. Although so far I had not had to pitch the room, I knew that my days of safety were numbered, which petrified me. I was rapidly becoming the Bott's lead cold caller. My leads were receptive when his account openers called them, and many opened accounts at Stratton. At the moment, I was his golden girl. But what would happen if I sucked at public speaking?

John pointed at Amy first. She stammered, stumbled, and giggled her way through her pitch. Soon it was my turn. Funny how I was so confident on the phone, but when I had to pitch to a group, especially my peers, it felt like volunteering for a firing squad. I thought about what my friend Pam had told me, and looked around the room at all the faces staring at me. I tried to imagine that I had, as she suggested, just given everyone there the best damn blow job ever. A sly grin spread across my face, and it all came together, so to speak. I did it. I got through it. The Bott gave me a thumbs-up, then cleared his throat and asked for attention.

"I'm going to leave you in the capable hands of John here, as I need to get ready for the deal that we are doing today. I am expecting to do a substantial amount of business," he said. "The company is called Octagon Engineering. It should do very well."

The first new issue since I'd arrived at Stratton Oakmont! Octagon's initial public offering traded as a unit. The units were bundles of stock that typically consisted of two warrants and two shares of common stock or a similar combination. Warrants were similar to options, and allowed buyers to purchase the stock at a special price. They were often included in deals to sweeten the pot. The number of warrants and stock that made up a unit was decided at the underwriter's discretion. The underwriter for Octagon, of course, was Stratton Oakmont.

I'll never forget the Octagon deal. The IPO price for a unit was $7 per share. The units took off within *minutes* of trading and immediately went north at the open. Pandemonium broke out in the room. Brokers were screaming, jumping on desks, and frantically trying to buy stock. The units closed on the first day of trading at $21. Clients had tripled their money in a single day! Frankie spoke about nothing else for the next six months. Every day it was drilled into our heads. *Octagon Octagon Octagon.*

"You guys can't imagine what's going on with this company. You do not own enough of this stock. There are things that I can say and things that I can't say, because of the Chinese wall that protects us all from conflicts of interest, but I *can* say that the company is poised for huge growth!"

I remember The Bott, who obediently bought a boatload of Octagon stock for his clients, telling me about a sign on the highway that happened to say Octagon. "Every day when I drive past that Octagon sign by LaGuardia Airport, I *bow*. I bow to the king!"

I was sold. I bought a thousand shares of the common stock for my personal account at $7 per share, not caring that it was a huge gamble for someone who was earning just $350 a week. Within the next few months, word on the street had it that Octagon was an unbelievable deal and no one could believe that Stratton Oakmont had been chosen to underwrite it. The story Frankie told us was this: Octagon was a waste management firm, based in Washington, DC, and run by a three-star general. Adler Coleman, Stratton Oakmont's clearing agent at the time, had introduced the two firms, based—they said—on Stratton Oakmont's past stellar performance with similar IPOs. But Octagon was more than a waste management company. It had also started a new division that was involved in the telecommunications sector, and was manufacturing a combination fax/phone/computer. Such a device was unique at the time and extremely desirable for the company's existing clients, particularly those in third-world countries. As a result, its stock was slowly heading north. The general was using his Pentagon contacts to develop new clients and to help Octagon attain a government-approved vendor status, which suggested that the company was poised for explosive growth.

New business was rolling in for the Bott. His clients loved him then. One thing I could say about the Bott was that he knew how to treat his employees. He caught up with me in the hallway one day. "Ginger, you are doing a great job. Your leads are super-receptive to our message, and we've opened a number of accounts from your leads. My team *loves* to pitch them Steven and I want to give you this as a little thank you!" He slipped me a crisp hundred-dollar bill. Steven was Steven Goldberg, the big schtocker in his group.

"Barry! Thank you so much! And please, say thank you to Steven, too!" He assured me that he would. Since most of the accounts that were opened from my leads were fairly new to the Bott, he did not offer the prospects IPO stock. But they were undoubtedly watching it triple and were counting the days before they could get the next new issue.

My $7,000 investment was soon worth $10,000. Frankie continued to push brokers to buy the stock, which wasn't hard to do. As he said, everyone loves to chase stock. Finally, the big news that Frankie had been promising us hit the tape. "Octagon received a $75 million order for its phone system." The stock flew to $14 per share. Before that deal, Octagon's revenues had been in the neighborhood of $25 million. That one order was worth triple the company's current revenue, which would certainly help light the fuse on that explosive growth that Frankie kept hinting at.

Several weeks later, Freddy called me at work to tell me that he had sold our position in Octagon. I was in shock. "You did *what?*"

"I sold the stock."

"You sold the stock. What were you *thinking?*"

"Babe, Ginger, didn't you see the article in the *Journal?*" I hadn't, but I snatched it up now. The article reported that reliable sources doubted the company's ability to write a contract as substantial as $75 million, and as information trickled in, the Journal was proven right. The contract that Octagon had received had been with a less-than-reputable firm that was back-dooring the sale for an end customer that was located in a country with a trade embargo forbidding any such dealings with the United States. The general had used a third party as a work-around! It was pretty sleazy!

Over the next few months, the stock went slowly down. Freddy and I had doubled our money, but most shareholders were not as fortunate. I wrote their losses off as nothing more than bad luck, greed, or being too dumb to sell the stock. After all, we were able to book a profit.

I didn't realize that I had started edging into that gray area, skirting the edge between right and wrong, good and bad. After all, that was the stock market. Sometimes people win and sometimes they lose.

The brainwashing continued.

Stratton fuckin' Oakmont! Stratton fuckin' Oakmont!

Stratton had an incredible sound system with speakers placed throughout the boardroom. There was no better way to brainwash the troops! Frankie used a mike to ensure that his message was heard loud and clear. The insane rah-rah meetings and abusive come-to-Jesus meetings continued, with very few speeches that were not one of the two extremes. It seemed that there was no middle of the road. The tone of the meeting depended on two things: whether or not the brokers appeared to have sat around all day doing nothing, and how stoned Frankie was. By that point, Frankie was stoned most of the time, so it was actually never a question of *if* anymore, only of "how bad is he today?"

In every meeting, twice a day, a good portion of what Frankie spoke about was getting rich. That was okay. That was why I was there, after all. It was pounded into our heads.

"At Stratton Oakmont, you have the opportunity to get *rich*." We were told this *every day*. "Stratton Oakmont is the best firm. We do the best deals. We've got the best brokers. You'll never make money anywhere else. If you leave here, you will end up working at McDonalds. We're *bad*. *We're Stratton fuckin' Oakmont!*"

⚬⚬⚬

I was becoming a great cold caller. I got ten leads, minimum, every day. The atmosphere was outrageously competitive, and in that male-dominated environment, the more macho guys couldn't handle getting their asses kicked by a woman. They were getting belligerent. I loved it. Men just hate to lose!

"Hey, Ginger, gimme me some of your leads. You have ten. The Bott won't miss one or two." It was the whiny ones I hated. They brought out my inner bitch.

"Get lost, creep. Learn your rebuttals and you'll be fine."

I used the exact same rebuttals that every other broker at Stratton Oakmont used, but I knew I had an edge. They were so much more powerful coming from a woman. I started thinking back to my Garment Center days, when I would give my forecast to the buyers in that same self-confident tone. I left them with no doubt who was in charge.

One of the reasons that I found cold calling so easy was that there were really only a few objections that the prospects ever used, and being armed with ready rebuttals took away the element of surprise. If customers said, "I don't buy stock," you came back with, "Who do you think you're kidding? I didn't get your name from the phone book." If customer said, "I'm not telling you how much I have in the market; that's personal," you came back with something like, "Yes, but I'm a broker, not your ex-wife's attorney." If customers didn't want to tell you the names of stocks they owned, you said, "Sir, I understand that you're a substantial investor, but I hardly think that if you tell me one stock, it will impact the Dow."

I really had my rebuttals down!

There was very little that someone could say to me that I did not have an answer for. I do remember one guy telling me that his wife was his broker, and unless I could cook and fuck like she did, he would not do business with me.

That caught me off guard, but I did say that I did not think that my husband would vouch for my *cooking*.

Another guy, when I asked how much he had in the market, shot back, "What's your cup size?"

"Excuse me?"

"Ginger, if you are going ask me something personal, then I want to know something personal, too."

"Okay…D."

He replied, "Three million."

I was an artist painting a picture. In my painting, Ginger Rogers had big breasts!

One of the ways Stratton Oakmont prepared its cold callers for the abuse that they would get on the phone was by doing skill-mills on a regular basis in the morning, and randomly after the market closed. The skill-mills trained us on the pitch and the rebuttals, and during them, every broker at Stratton Oakmont was required to pitch the room. I've read that the most common fear people have is a fear of public speaking. In other words, they are less afraid of dying than of talking in front of a group of people. I had the same fear, but I was getting better, slowly. But it was a reasonable thing to be a little anxious about pitching a room full of five hundred to a thousand wild animals just waiting for you to mess up.

Everybody in the room, including me, practically drooled when someone in the herd stumbled. Some, smelling blood and weakness, went in for the kill: "You fuckin' idiot. No wonder you don't open any accounts!" "I have never seen such a worthless piece of shit. Why don't you get the fuck out of here and go work at Burger King?" "At Stratton Oakmont, we spend hours and hours of our time trying to help you be successful. If you don't even have the fuckin' decency to learn this two-minute pitch, then maybe you should consider another line of work!" "At Stratton Oakmont, we do the best deals!" "Stratton fuckin' Oakmont!"

I was getting better and better at pitching the room. I always knew the lines, but sometimes I still froze up and blanked out. Fortunately, the Bott was not interested in making his team look like shit, so he rarely called on me. There were lots of benefits working for Barry Bottswoth. The Bott was one of the biggest producers in the firm—at least, his group was one of the biggest producers. His partner, Steven Goldberg, was the big schtocker on the team, and the Bott managed the staff. The Bott and Steve's group usually consisted of five to ten cold callers, three to six account openers, and a sales assistant. The Bott also managed the entire cold calling section, hiring recruits, assigning them to brokers, and holding training and motivational meetings. The Bott never actually trained anyone personally, but he always made sure that we had as much training as we needed to be successful. He would not tolerate losers on the team. The Bott took good care of his best employees, the ones who worked hard and produced. He was very fair and generous if you did your job.

Several weeks after I started at Stratton Oakmont, I mentioned to the Bott that my friend Neil Hautz had an account with the firm, with some guy named Glen Polanski. The Bott grew excited. He told me to follow him and that he wanted to introduce me to Glen, who was one of the principals of the firm. We went into the private office that Glen shared with Josh Shamus.

I had seen Glen give an occasional meeting to the boardroom and noticed that in addition to being a good speaker, he was really kind of good looking. Very sexy, as a matter of fact. Glen was tall with dark black hair that he wore slightly long in the back to compensate for the fact that he was going bald in the front. The hair plugs that were evident in the front told me that hair loss was an issue with him. His body had been carefully sculpted in the gym—and the sculptor was definitely and artist. What a body! Glen exuded a definite animal magnetism and, like Frankie, he knew how to get the room going, though with slightly more savoir faire.

The Bott introduced me. "Glen, I want to introduce you to my star cold caller, Ginger Rogers."

I surprised Glen by marching up to his desk and thrusting out my hand. "Glen, it's nice to finally meet you. I've heard so much about you! We have a mutual friend."

The Bott saw that he had caught Glen off guard. "She's a friend of Neil Hautz," he said.

I smiled, looked Glen in the eyes and added in my throaty, sexy voice, "Neil tells me that you are a wonderful broker."

Glen was speechless. I gathered that he was not used to dealing with self-confident women. What really seemed to shock him was the fact that I was a cold caller. He did not respond directly to me, but turned to Josh. Josh looked at Glen. They both turned to the Bott and said, in unison, "*She's working for us.*"

I never did work for Glen, of course, but I thought that the obvious power struggle that was going on there was hilarious. There was no way that the Bott was going to let me work for someone else, even the principals. My leads easily translated into new accounts, and new accounts were what made brokers rich. That was what Frankie said.

The longer I worked at Stratton Oakmont, the more that I began to realize that I was surrounded by a bunch of very strange men. There was one group of young men, more like boys actually, that sat behind me. I was certain that no one in that group had ever worked in a serious job before. Maybe they were diamonds in the rough, but they were *so* rough that so far very little brilliance had shone through.

We actually had a dress code at Stratton Oakmont. All male brokers and trainees were required to wear a white shirt and a tie. One of the rough diamonds sauntered in on day in a madras shirt sans tie, perhaps because there was possibly no tie in existence that would improve the look of that loud, ugly, shirt. Glen tapped him on the shoulder and asked him, in full view of the others, "Anderson, what is the dress code here?"

"A white shirt and tie."

"Is that a white shirt? Are you wearing an invisible tie?"

"No, sir."

"Okay, so you do know that you're in violation. I really don't want to send you home. What's your excuse?"

"My white shirts were all dirty. I stayed here late last night, and then I rushed back here this morning. I wanted to be on time this morning, and this was the only clean shirt I could find. And seriously, I figured with this shirt, wearing a tie would be worse than not wearing one."

Great answer! The kid could think on his feet.

Glen let him off with a warning. "Don't let it happen again."

I thought of my husband leaving for his job at AIG. My darling, sweet Freddy. Forced to choose, Freddy would leave his pants home rather than show up without a tie. I laughed to myself.

The rough diamonds grew more outrageous every day. First they learned my phone extension, and called it surreptitiously throughout meetings. Then they started bombarding me with spitballs and rubber bands. What kind of place did they think they were working at? I tried to ignore them, but that only made them bolder. At first, I thought they were flirting, but I eventually realized that they were jealous of my skills—as if I could help that I was a natural-born star. Still, I considered them harmless enough until the day that I overheard a conversation.

I hated to snitch, but I had to tell the Bott. "I overheard Jay talking with the guys about his ex-girlfriend. I don't know what the hell happened between the two of them, or what she did to him, but he was more than just upset. He was at his desk in a complete rage! He was telling Stu his plan for revenge against this girl," I said, shivering. "He's decided to send her a dead chicken, minus its head. This is really over the top."

The Bott stared at me. "Anything else?"

"Yeah. Stu said to Jay, 'Joey says to pick him up Saturday at seven o'clock. He has this butcher friend that can get us as many dead chickens as we need.' And Jay said, 'I would really love to see that cunt's face when she opens the door and she sees a fuckin' decapitated chicken! That bitch will get what she deserves.' But Jay wasn't done yet. He wanted to know if Stu thought they could get into the girl Cindy's bedroom and leave the bloody head under her pillow."

I'd stopped listening at that point, and gone to see the Bott. I was really a little scared by their reveling in all the gory details. But the Bott refused to fire the hoodlums, claiming that he wanted to give them the benefit of the doubt. It wasn't easy to get cold callers. And he was right; they hadn't really done any-thing to get fired, but I couldn't help thinking that it was just a matter of time. In the meantime, I was thankful that all I was finding were spitballs, and not bloody chicken heads.

Yet every day that the young hoodlums worked at Stratton Oakmont, they did something bolder and more outrageous than the day before. When one of the female brokers, May Steiner, was asked to give a training meeting, the rough diamond cold callers arranged for special seat just for her. The guy that set it up was an overweight, beefy mess of a man. When May approached the group, he was finishing up his lunch and still had a half-eaten apple in his mouth. His resemblance to a giant hog being roasted on a spit was uncanny, and at first May giggled at his antics. But then the others announced that the Queen of the May had been given a special throne befitting her beauty and talents, and she stopped laughing. Her throne was an upside down trash can, covered with scraps of toilet paper and mounds of peanut butter shaped to look like turds. At least, I hoped it was peanut butter. I left the room.

I was starting to believe that I was working not in a brokerage but at some sort of loony bin. The guys shouted intimate details of their sex lives from one desk to another as if it were nothing. I did not need to know that one of them had masturbated on his living room sofa so much that he had to throw out the blanket he'd used to cover it. I tried to block such things out by muttering sarcastic comments to myself: "Well, thank God he didn't ruin the sofa!"

When I complained to the Bott about them again, Randy Cohen, who was one of the brokers who had hired the creeps, looked at me with disgust. "Can you please shut your uterus?"

I was almost stunned into silence, but I recovered quickly. "Fuck off, Randy. It's not open for you, anyway."

Although I complained repeatedly, there was little that could be done, as they were never really caught being anything but obnoxious. That is, until they finally went too far, and took Randy Cohen's Ferrari for a joyride. I hoped they had used it to deliver bloody poultry.

A month after I started working at Stratton Oakmont, someone showed me an article about the problems that the firm was having with the SEC. We had apparently just been fined $2 million dollars for trading violations, which Stratton Oakmont had paid without admitting or denying guilt. Two principals I didn't know had been forced to resign and had been banned from the securities industry for life. Frankie somehow managed to avoid losing his license, but his Series 24, or manager's license, was suspended for one year. In Frankie's mind, the suspension simply meant that he temporarily couldn't sign tickets.

In the 90's the trading window required all tickets be signed by a principal of the firm. A trade was filled by walking it over to the trading window. If there was a line at the window, too bad! We waited our turns. That is, some of us did. The men never followed the rules because they were so much bigger than the women. They would cut the line or yell over the women's heads as if they were not even there. Their buys were always more important than whatver the women had going on.

When I had passed my Series 7, I would show them who ruled!

Other than Frankie losing his ability to sign tickets, nothing else changed as far as I could see. Well, almost nothing. Stratton Oakmont was thereafter required to host an independent team of advisers from the SEC. A brokerage firm knew it was in trouble when it was forced to host the SEC. The stock market was policed in 1994 by the NASD. Although it acted as though it was a government agency, NASD was a private corporation. Its later incarnation and successor, the Financial Industry Regulatory Authority or FINRA, was also a self-regulated organization. It was formed after NASD blew up in the late 1990s.

Now, I wouldn't want to be quoted as saying that there was a connection between NASD's implosion and Stratton Oakmont's demise in 1996, but it does seem a little incredible to think that anyone seriously thought that a so-called self-regulatory organization could remain honest, ethical, and impartial when it was surrounded by the daily temptations that were part of the brokerage world. They weren't completely without oversight, however. Above them was an actual government organization: the Securities and Exchange Commission. Nobody wanted to mess with the SEC.

It was a little disconcerting, and at the same time comforting, to have the SEC camped in our offices. I was concerned about what was going on at Stratton Oakmont, but I wasn't really sure if asking questions was wise. The Bott came to the rescue. He had obviously seen the articles and heard all the scuttlebutt, and his rebuttals were brilliant.

"This is the most highly regulated industry in the world—more so than the nuclear power industry. The NASD and the SEC *look* for problems in the industry; that's what they do; it's their job to spot things that seem out of the ordinary. There isn't a day that goes by that one brokerage firm or another isn't fined for something—look at Prudential and its limited partnership fiasco. Every firm has its problems."

The SEC made some suggestions, and the changes were immediately implemented. Frankie explained in his next meeting. "Hey, guys. Listen up. As you know, we have some guests here from the SEC. They have taken a look at our business practices and have asked us to make some changes," he said.

"They have a problem with baseless price predictions. You are not allowed to guarantee that the stock will go up. Not that *anyone* did before." A ripple of laughter crossed the room and died down when people remembered that the "guests" were still in the room *with* us. "More importantly, we cannot even *strongly suggest* that it will go up. We cannot offer a stop-loss on NASDAQ stocks that we recommend. My goal is to make Stratton Oakmont the most compliant firm on the street."

That's what Frankie *said*.

In reality, the only change he actually made was that we were now required to record all calls. I didn't have a problem with Stratton Oakmont recording my calls—it even saved me several times—but I'm pretty sure that I was in the minority of brokers that felt this way.

The brokers at Stratton Oakmont often told customers that they would watch the stock and give them a virtual stop-loss. That was completely illegal. "If this stock ticks down a quarter, I'm on the phone with you!" they assured their clients. What they failed to add was that we couldn't sell the stock even if we wanted to, which is why some brokers rationalized that it was okay. They considered it a white lie in a gray area, telling customers that they had a stop-loss when they had no such protection. It was only after they hung up that the brokers would chuckle out loud, "Yeah, I'll call ya…but you ain't selling *shit*."

Our conversations were all carefully monitored. But brokers at Stratton Oakmont who were caught in-house committing any of these violations would, in the worst-case scenario, get a slap on the wrist. Yet even that reassured me that Stratton Oakmont was on the up-and-up. When Frankie told us that we would become the most compliant firm on the street, I believed him! I wanted to believe him. That's the scary part. There was always an element of truth in what was said to us, enough to convince us that it was senseless to worry.

The "guests" snooped around almost every day. They occasionally interviewed brokers and cold callers. Stratton Oakmont wanted me to meet with them because I was the straightest person in the room and spoke fairly well. Most of the guys in the room thought of me as a schoolteacher type who would definitely make a good impression.

I was terrified.

I knew what we'd been told was legal or not legal, but I had never verified any of it. Like most people there, I was relying on others' generally self-serving interpretations. For example, we were told that the laws in New York required the consent of only one party to record a conversation. Since the brokers consented, that met the requirements, so we rarely disclosed to customers that a call was being recorded. I was told it was legal, but I didn't know for sure.

I approached the interview with trepidation. To me, good impressions notwithstanding, I was not a good choice to talk to the SEC. I was too new and I couldn't answer even basic questions about the market. I prayed that they would not get into specifics about Big Board this and OTC that. I put on my game face and cautiously approached the room where the snoops were camped out. I was surprised to see two middle-aged, totally average men. Frick and Frack were nothing like the sharks that I had expected to meet. They were dressed exactly the same, wearing dark, cheap suits, wrinkled white shirts with slightly frayed collars, and pastel polyester foulard ties. Their shoes were definitely Thom McAn, their watches Timex. They were not a pretty sight.

"You must be Ginger Rogers. Please come in."

I sat in front of the two bozos, wondering why the room was twenty-five degrees colder than any other place at Stratton Oakmont. Others had joked that it was a common sign of paranormal activity, but I suspected the real reason was much more conventional: Frankie was hoping to shorten their visit by freezing them out. It didn't appear to be working. My interview with them lasted more than thirty minutes. I was shivering by the end, but Frick and Frack seemed completely unaffected.

The SEC investigators asked many less-than-memorable questions, most of which related to how I spent a typical day at Stratton Oakmont. "Ginger, are you familiar with the SEC?" they asked. "Do you know who we are?"

"Well, yes, sure. I believe I am familiar."

"Good! The SEC was created in 1934 . WE are dedicated to protecting investors and the public from unethical behavior. President Roosevelt appointed Joseph P. Kennedy Sr., father of President John F. Kennedy, to serve as the first commissioner of the SEC," said Frick. "People found that ironic since Joe Kennedy had made a fortune in the stock market by taking advantage of some of the very laxities that the new SEC was tightening up—the classic fox guarding the henhouse. Anyway, we are the government agency responsible for policing the stock market."

"Oh, okay."

"We are here at Stratton Oakmont to review cold-calling techniques, taping requirements, trading, and sales," said Frack. "We'd like to review your cold-calling technique. Can you pitch us?"

I couldn't believe that I was so comfortable with the guy. I had no problem pitching him.

"Good morning, Mr. Jones? This is Ginger Rogers from Stratton Oakmont. How are you today?"

"Dandy," said Frack.

"I am with Stratton Oakmont. Have you heard of my firm? We are one of the leading NASDAQ underwriters in the country," I said. "The reason I'm calling is that I would like to send you information on my firm and, down the road, maybe share an idea. Fair enough?"

"Not interested," said Frack.

"I understand that you are not interested. Thanks, anyway. Have a nice day." I pantomimed hanging up a phone.

Frick and Frack had spent a great deal of time as the firm's "guests" by that time, so I knew they had heard Frankie's explosive morning-meeting rants. But if they were expecting me to call my "client" a piker midget asshole and threaten to rip his face off, they would have to be disappointed. I wasn't about to vary from my innocuous and carefully developed pitch, the one I used hundreds of times a day. But what I said on the phone, and what others said on the phone—and what Frankie allowed everyone to say on the phone—were all very different things.

Still, the practiced, smooth way I delivered my pitch seemed to have convinced the two bozos that there was a clean, compliant script that we all followed faithfully. The guys sitting across from me actually believed me. And why wouldn't they, when I spoke with such conviction? It was all coming together for me. When I spoke with conviction, I could sell someone the Brooklyn Bridge. Frick and Frack were sold. Better yet, they were my new best friends.

I imagined Frankie sitting in his office smoking a doob, listening to my bullshit and laughing his ass off. (I didn't know at the time that Frankie had bugged the room and that he and Jared, another owner, *were* in fact listening to every word.) But he could laugh all he wanted. I had not betrayed the precious family. Good thing I was a loyal Strattonite!

Frick asked me one question that was, in retrospect, laughable beyond belief—not because of what they asked or my response, but because of *their* response to me. "Ginger, do you think that Stratton Oakmont has changed its ways here and become compliant? What we want to know is, do you feel that management is making a concerted effort to change?"

"Oh, yes! Absolutely! They are *very* concerned about being compliant. We've received numerous training sessions on what we can and cannot say. The firm is monitoring trades, and compliance reviews every large trade." I was certain that I should be nominated for an academy award, because my performance with those two was spectacular!

Frick and Frack leaned back with satisfied smiles. "We totally agree with you. We have seen a tremendous change in the environment in the last few months."

That was not what I expected. They *agreed* with me? Couldn't they see what was going on? They had been there for weeks on end—watching, listening, reviewing—and they didn't see what was happening? Did I have to spell it out for them? The truth was that although compliance reviewed every large trade, the rogue brokers were not disciplined by Stratton Oakmont.

On the surface, Stratton Oakmont was compliant. We changed one or two aspects of how the brokers traded—the scripts really bothered the SEC—but nothing major had been altered. I could only assume that the two guys were not too sharp. I should have known when I realized that they really thought that there was a problem with the heat in just that one room. Come on—even I figured that one out.

As it turned out, I was the one who was not too sharp. I didn't figure out until much later that they were quietly on the Stratton Oakmont payroll. The fox guarding the henhouse, indeed.

Frankie's meetings continued to pound his message. "We're the best brokerage firm in the country. We do the best deals. We're a family. We'll take care of you. You'll never make money anywhere else. You have the chance to get *rich* at Stratton Oakmont. LIQUID! Imagine, $100k in the bank. At Stratton Oakmont, we work hard, play hard. *Work hard, play hard. Work hard, play hard.*

It's not easy, but it's simple. Just pick up the phone. *Just pick up the fuckin' phone!*"

My favorite was the Pinto slam. "If you leave Stratton Oakmont, one day, as you're tooling around town in your Pinto, you'll pull up next to a Ferrari with a beautiful blonde in the passenger seat. You'll notice that the driver looks familiar. '*Oh, yeah*, that was the guy sitting next to me at Stratton Oakmont.' And you'll look at your fat, ugly wife, and your kid picking his nose, and you'll think, 'That could have been me!'"

I was beginning to think that instead of its wimpy advisers, the SEC should have sent in a team of psychiatrists. Perhaps they could have found a group of doctors familiar with cults and brainwashing techniques. The handwriting was on the wall in 1996 when we were given a new cold-calling rule that required NASD member firms to keep "do not call" lists of persons who did not wish to receive telephone solicitations of any sort. Certain changes prohibited brokers from calling individuals' residences to sell securities during certain times, unless they had the prior consent of the person. In addition, they were required to give their names, the name of their firms, their telephone number or address, and state the purpose of the call.

I imagined calls something like this: "Hello, Mr. Jones. This is Ginger Rogers with Stratton Oakmont, located at 1979 Marcus Avenue in beautiful Lake Success. I'm calling to sell you some dog-shit stock."

CLICK.

Neither my husband nor my friends understood why I continued to work there. Sometimes I asked myself why I stayed, but I knew the answer. Because I *believed*. I bought what they were selling.

Stratton Oakmont was built on a dream. Well, it turned out to have been a mentally disturbed, misguided dream—more like a nightmare—but it started as a dream. And the owners spent every day making us believers of that dream. I'm sure that the millions of dollars that they pocketed helped them maintain their unbridled enthusiasm. Frankie Porter, it was rumored, was worth $50 or $60 million. Jared Bellmore, the original owner and brains behind Stratton Oakmont, was rumored to be worth $200 million.

Later Jared claimed that he would give up all his money to have his license back. That's hard to believe, considering the fact that he *had* made the concept of Stratton Oakmont work for him. Where else could a short, skinny, totally average Jewish kid from Queens amass that kind of wealth? Jared was a street hustler who figured out a way to beat the system. Everyone said that he was an unbelievable salesman, starting with his early days selling steaks off the back of a truck and ending with his expulsion from the securities industry. It's said that Jared was the person who developed the Stratton Oakmont machine. Although he was banned from the business, he continued to profit from his shares in the firm for several years after he lost his license. Every prospectus that I read disclosed the fact that Jared Bellmore was involved in the private placement or bridge loan to whatever company Stratton brought public. Those were short-term loans to companies prior to their public offering. They were extremely profitable.

Several brokers were brought up on charges for selling investments without disclosing that they were speculative or the fact that Jared Bellmore was involved. The Stratton attorney representing them went to the trial with the prospectus blown up to poster size, clearly showing that this information had been disclosed. However, just as the firm's "welcome aboard" letter was routinely ignored, so were the prospectuses. Most investors never bothered to read them.

Most Stratton Oakmont investors in private placements—we called them privates—made ten times their original investment within nine to twelve months. Needless to say, privates were only offered to very wealthy clients, friends, and Jared Bellmore. Jared made several million dollars *every time* Stratton did a deal. With most privates, investors could only sell stock at the underwriter's discretion prior to the one-year holding period. That was not usually a problem at Stratton Oakmont. Their IPOs usually traded in high volume at the open. Liquidity was not an issue for the elite customers that opted to lock in their profit. Our brokers were there to provide that liquidity. When management at Stratton Oakmont told us to push a certain stock, it was because *they were the ones selling it.* Jared had this all figured out. He also figured out that the way to have brokers do whatever he wanted was to hire brokers with no experience, train them to do everything his way, make the firm a fun place to work, and pay them lots of money. It worked like a charm.

Brokers at Stratton Oakmont *did* make a lot of money, although a lot of them spent it as fast as they made it. This was pushed by management at every meeting. That's not surprising, since so many of the brokers were young and single. Earning two, three, or five hundred thousand a year when they were barely old enough to drink legally was too much for most of them to handle responsibly. It didn't help them that the atmosphere at Stratton Oakmont encouraged this extravagance. The preferred car was a Ferrari, the favorite watch was a Rolex, and the drug of choice was cocaine. Strattonnites were encouraged to party hard. *Work hard, play hard.* And spend money as fast as they made it.

My favorite part of the month was the last day of the pay period. The brokers were required to stand and announce to the room exactly how much they had grossed. Of course, everyone lied, but even considering the brokers' fudge factor, it was still a lot of money. The Bott and Steven made unbelievable amounts of money. I can remember months when they grossed $700,000. With a 50 percent payout, that would translate to $175,000 each—for one month's work.

Fortunately for me, the Bott knew the value of good employees, so he had no problem throwing me a *hunge* every now and then. Those hundred-dollar bonuses were one of the reasons I loved working for him. The Bott knew that I couldn't survive a cold caller's salary. And it was peanuts to him. The Bott giving me a hundred dollars was like me giving my housekeeper ten cents. It meant absolutely nothing to him.

Every broker at Stratton Oakmont flashed money around. The culture there encouraged it. Josh Shamus, to prove to his trainees how much money he made, started tearing up hundred-dollar bills and throwing the pieces at us, shouting, "You can be *rich* at Stratton Oakmont!"

Jared once paid a sales assistant who was vain about her hair ten grand to have her head shaved in the boardroom. TEN THOUSAND DOLLARS!

Of course, for ten thousand dollars I would have let them shave any part of my body. Money: that's what it was all about. *You, too, can be rich! Follow me. Do what I say. You will be rich.*

───── ◦◦◦◦ ─────

Six weeks after starting at Stratton Oakmont, I started the hardest part of becoming a broker. I was given my Series 7 books. Stratton Oakmont wanted to have a constant flow of new, inexperienced, specially trained brokers, so the firm sponsored trainees and provided them with the books and the classes required to get a Series 7 license, as did every other brokerage. Trainees who passed the test on their first attempt had all related costs covered by the firm. I was determined to pass the exam on the first time. Freddy and I had not paid the ski house mortgage in two months, and there was no way I was paying to take the test. Not that I had a clue how much the test cost. It didn't matter. I was determined to pass it as quickly as possible. I was anxious to go on my own and make some real money.

I thought that the Bott would be pleased at the thought of me becoming a broker, but good cold callers were hard to get, so he seemed to have mixed emotions. He knew that it was the beginning of the end of our relationship. I was truly the best cold caller that he had ever had. Not only did I work my ass off, bringing in tons of leads, but those leads continued to be receptive and translated into accounts that traded. That equaled gross.

I could tell that the Bott hoped to keep me a little longer by the way he encouraged me to work late and keep my studying to a minimum, but I was on a mission. I *had* to pass the test. I was always a great test taker, so I wasn't too concerned. My goal was to take and pass the test in the shortest amount of time humanly possible. That would not be easy. The Series 7 material is extremely boring as well as voluminous, a wonderful book for treating insomnia. The Series 7 test has been called the third-hardest state exam, after the bar and CPA exams.

For several weeks after I received the Series 7 materials, when I wasn't actively cold calling I tuned out completely and buried myself in my studies. Stratton Oakmont had an internal test that I needed to pass before the firm would send me to the state-sponsored test prep class to study. This was Frankie's way of weeding out what he called the 'tards from those who actually had a shot at passing the exam. I was so nervous just taking the stupid Stratton Oakmont test that I was certain that I didn't score well. I wasn't even sure that I passed it. I did.

It probably didn't really matter what we scored on the internal exam; it was simply the way the firm moved us through the system. And the next step for me was the prep class. Given by a wonderful teacher at Hofstra University, the class was actually very helpful and professional. Since most of the trainees from

Stratton Oakmont, including me, continued working full time while studying for their Series 7, we were not exactly at our sharpest in the evening classes.

The biggest problem that I had with the class was that the students were all on different levels in terms of their knowledge and understanding of the material. The instructor looked at me one night, having seen the disgusted look on my face. "Ginger, are you getting this?"

Yeah, I got it three weeks ago. Let's move on. Was I in the remedial class? After the prep class, we were sent home to study for the Series 7 exam.

My biggest fear in taking the Series 7 was that I would not be able to sleep the night before. I feared that I would be so nervous that I would be up all night worrying. Today I would have taken an Ambien, but at that time, that delightful pill was not yet on the market. When the time came, I just had to tough it out. I knew I was as prepared as I could be, and on track to become a broker in record time, and I slept like a baby the night before the test.

On the day of the test, I was pretty excited. It was do or die time. I was ready. Come on, let's do it! The Series 7 exam is a currently given by FINRA. Once I had my Series 7 license, I could make different types of trades with all types of corporate securities. It would also let me take other exams for higher-level certifications, but for now I was looking at one exam with two hundred fifty scored questions and ten unscored questions being evaluated for future use. A passing grade was one hundred eighty correct answers, or 72 percent.

The test was held in a very basic, nondescript room. The security seemed fairly tight. The test was computer-based, and each test was configured differently with the same material but in a different order, so even someone inclined to cheat would not be able to copy answers off a neighboring screen. The testing center supplied scratch paper, pencils, and basic electronic calculators; everything had to be returned at the end of the test. We were not allowed to bring anything of our own. We were also given an *Exhibits* book that showed charts, graphs, tables or scenarios referenced in some of the questions. We had to return those after the test, too.

The good thing about the computer-based test was that it would allow me to receive a report of my test results on the same day I took the test. The report would tell anyone taking the test whether or not they passed, their score, and a profile showing their performance with respect to the major job functions covered on the exam. When I finished taking the test, I would know where I did well—and where I sucked. It was an easy way of highlighting what new brokers might want to do, or avoid: candidates who were really bad in math, for example, might find that they did not do well on the questions relating to puts and calls.

If I failed the test, the report would let me see where I needed to study more for next time. But I was determined that I would not need a next time. I dove nervously into Part One and, to my surprise and dismay, finished it much faster than I had projected. That worried me. The test just seemed too easy. What I figured out as I went through the test really shocked me.

When I initially started studying for the Series 7, one of the brokers at Stratton Oakmont suggested that I study for it by taking practice exams. I bought a book of them at the stationery store. The book contained a dozen or so exams that became progressively more difficult. After reading through the initial course study material, I put that book away and never opened it again. That was a shame, because I had so enjoyed reading about the fictitious firm of Beat-um, Cheat-um, and Fleece-um! I spent a week focusing on the practice exams. I took each test maybe three times until I had passed all the practice tests.

As I began taking the actual test, I realized that many of the questions were similar to the questions on the practice exam, which helped me breeze through the material. The more questions I completed, the more comfortable I became, and I felt certain that my answers were correct. Then I again started to get scared. The test seemed *too* easy. Something was wrong. I wasn't sure what, though, so I reviewed all the questions on Part One yet again before I took the required lunch break.

I thought about going back after lunch and once more rechecking my answers, but soon learned that that wouldn't be possible. Once I broke for lunch, it was what it was. There would be no more revisiting the first half. I calmed myself by reassuring myself that I would do better on the second part, the section dealing with options. This involved puts and calls, in the money, out of the money. Most of the brokers I knew were bad at math and many brokers never sold options, so consequently many candidates just barely passed the exam. I was fairly confident that the section would not pose a problem for me, though, as I had always been an A student in math.

I spotted another Stratton Oakmont broker wannabe at lunch. She called me over. "Hey, Ginger. Come sit here."

"Hi, Susan! How ya doin'? Wow, this food looks awful!"

"It *is* pretty bad," she said. "But after sitting inside for four hours taking a test, I am so hungry that I would eat anything right now. I can't believe how hard my test was. I'm sure I didn't do well. How was yours?"

"Oh? I don't know. It seemed a little too easy," I said. "I breezed right through it in three hours and sat there for an hour twiddling my thumbs. The security here is ridiculous!"

"You didn't think the test was hard?"

"Well, I studied a lot for it. The second half will probably be harder. Part Two of the test is all on options."

Susan rolled her eyes. "Great." I found out later that Susan got a forty-three on the test.

While I waited for Part Two to begin, I began to wonder if Part One had consisted of trick questions. Was it possible that I had not understood them at all? The practice exams had contained many subtle trick questions that had been easy to get wrong if I read the question too quickly. But Part Two of the test left me feeling exactly the same way. It went by even faster.

Then it hit me. It was like a light bulb turned on inside my brain! The questions on the exam were not similar to the questions on the practice exams. They were *exactly* the same questions. I figured it out when I got to a question on options that required calculating an answer. When I saw the question, I could not believe it! The numbers were exactly the same! I didn't even have to do the math, because I remembered the question and the correct answer. I breezed through the second half of the exam. After five hours of testing, I was done—in every sense. I couldn't sit there another minute and check and recheck what I was sure now was a passing test. I decided to finish up and see how I had done.

Once I completed every question and indicated that I was ready to quit taking the test, the computer asked me to confirm. "Are you SURE you want to quit?" Well, thank you for asking, Mr. Computer, but yes, I am sure I would like to quit. I clicked on YES and waited for my score. And waited. The six-hour test seemed to have gone by faster than the thirty seconds it took the computer to calculate my score and produce my report. Finally, some numbers appeared, but I could not see my score. It took several minutes to sink in. The ninety-two on the screen *was* my score. I got a fuckin' ninety-two on my Series 7! Wahooo! The average score nationwide for the test was seventy-six, which is why I was so confused seeing just ninety-two flashing across the screen. I kept thinking, *I see a 92, but where is my grade?* I had not only passed, I had aced the damn test!

I had never failed a test in my life, so I wasn't surprised that I had passed the Series 7. I was, however, surprised that I had excelled. It was almost like taking a foreign language and getting an A on the first test. I had known going in that I understood most of the information, but I couldn't believe how *easily* I mastered it.

The next few weeks were going to be hell. I needed to transition from being a cold caller to becoming an account opener. I was determined to get through it. What I found really strange was that when I asked the Bott a question about the market, he wouldn't give me a straight answer.

"Hey, Mister Bott Man, I have a question."

"Yes, Ginger?"

"What's a Fibonacci number?"

"I'll tell you in one minute. Hold on." The Bott went into his office, grabbed a book off his desk, and was back in the boardroom before I even had a chance to sit down.

"I don't have the time to explain this to you, but you can look it up." He tossed the book on my desk and then disappeared into his office, shutting the door behind him. I wasn't surprised. He had done the same thing to me before—tell me that he was too busy to answer a question, and recommend that I look it up. Several years later, I learned that the reason that the Bott blew off my questions repeatedly. *He did not know the answers*. It didn't matter what the question was, because the Bott knew *nothing* about the stock market. He had paid his brother-in-law to take not only his Series 7 exam, but his Series 24 exam, the one that allowed him to become a principal of the firm. He cheated.

I, however, had studied and passed my Series 7, and done incredibly well on it. So well that I could even use my new status itself as a rebuttal. "Mr. Jones, I understand that you want to think about buying this stock. But do you really think that your [attorney or accountant or stockbroker] could pass his [bar or CPA or Series 7] exam if he had to take it tomorrow? I assure you that he *could not.* I'm not saying the he's a bad [attorney or accountant or stockbroker]. I'm saying that the time to make a decision is when the facts are fresh in your mind!"

I found the new information and new world that I was about to enter fascinating and compelling. The job was so different from anything that I had ever done before or even thought about doing before. When stocks were running, whether up or down, I couldn't imagine having a more exciting job.

Bring it on! I'm bad! I'm a Stratton Oakmont broker!

When I found out that I had aced my Series 7, it was June 20th, 1994. I was ready and pumped. I had left the testing facility prepared for anything and everything. I couldn't wait to tell the Bott. The next day, Tuesday, was an absolutely beautiful, end of June- beginning of summer, New York type of day. When I got to Stratton Oakmont, I ran straight into the Bott's office. I may be exaggerating to say that I ran, but if anyone had gotten in front of me I would have knocked them over in my rush to share the good news. I burst into the Bott's office and announced to the Bott and everyone in his office:

"Hey, Bott! I passed—with a ninety-two!"

I knew that for the Bott, my news meant losing a great cold caller, but he would be gaining a phenomenal account opener. His face reflected mixed feelings. "Come with me," he said. He led me to Glen Polansky's office.

I felt Glen's eyes undress me as I walked in the room. Did he do that to every woman who walked in? My guess was that he was a dirt-bag, a big-time womanizer. And yet…there was something so hot about him.

I looked around. The office he shared with Josh. It was on the outside wall of the building, located off the center of the boardroom—strategically placed to view and monitor the brokers. On the wall separating the office from the boardroom, there were three large interior windows with the kind of cheap, tacky, horizontal blinds that my client, Dr. Ebert, would have loved to have used to demonstrate his cleaning solution—and should have, considering how much they needed a good cleaning. Glen and Josh could check out the boardroom action, or lack of action, without leaving their desks. They both had giant mahogany desks—one neat, and the other fairly messy. There was a wall hook seemingly randomly placed into one wall; it held an assortment of newly cleaned and pressed clothing. The room was cluttered with piles of prospectuses, trading tickets, and personal items. Glen's neater half of the room held the usual collection of photos. I assumed that the ugly bitch in one of them was Glen's wife. Although she actually looked hot in the picture, I had seen her in the office. Some women just photograph well.

"I got a ninety-two on my Series 7!" I burst out without preamble.

Glen looked over at Josh, who was sitting behind the messiest desk that I had ever seen. They both turned to the Bott and said, in unison, "She's working for us!"

The Bott ignored them once again.. They just wanted to stick it to him, it seemed, for they said this same thing every time he and I entered their office together. But I knew that he wasn't about to let his star player join another team. I heard Josh mutter to Glen something to the effect that I had "studied too hard."

When we returned to the main room, I heard several other trainees reporting their test scores to the Bott. Sal admitted sheepishly that he had just barely passed his test, scoring only a seventy-three. The Bott had a point to make. "Listen up, everybody! Listen up! Sal got a hundred on his Series 7 test!" The Bott turned to the bewildered Sal and explained. "This isn't Harvard. You passed. the test. As far as I am concerned, seventy-three is as good as a hundred."

That said it all. And it really *was* as good, once I thought about it. No one would ever ask. The license was what was important, not the score. That type of logic set the tone for my behavior over the next six months.

Word of my score, however, had leaked out. Several of the men who had failed the test or barely passed wouldn't even look me in the eye, though I could imagine what they were doing and saying behind my back. Josh and Glen did not appear especially happy at having been blown away by a "blond bimbo." I can only imagine their scores! *Too damn bad.* They would have to get over it.

Now that I had my license, I could officially move to the Bott's area in the brokers' half of the boardroom. I wanted to do it immediately. There was something extremely motivational about being able to move my seat past the poles. Well, it was not just about moving. Trainees worked wherever they could find an unoccupied space in the back of the room. Up front, I would actually have a desk that I could call my own, along with my own a phone—and a Quotron!

The room divided the "scum of the earth" cold callers from the wonderful and respected brokers, the losers from the winners, the moneymakers from the poor. I was so close to making money that I could taste it. I was now the Bott's account opener, and I would be near him and the brokers on his team.

The Bott's account opening program was as rigid as his cold-calling program had been. I was expected to be in work by eight o'clock and to stay at work as late as possible. I still had to make cold calls, but once I had built up a lead base of two hundred qualified prospects, the Bott would return the leads to me. Then I could try to open those leads into accounts.

I had been warned that all brokers were slime, so I copied all the leads that I got before I gave them to the Bott, just in case. And he knew that all account openers were thieving bastards, so he insisted on keeping the lead base in his office. Stratton Oakmont was just like a family—a dysfunctional family, at best, but a family. What a great relationshipthe Bott and I shared, one based on total mistrust!

Any new account that was opened had to be approved by a principal of the firm. To be approved, the client had to have at least $100,000 in the market (experienced investor), an annual income of $100,000 (qualified), a net worth of $1,000,000 (wealthy), and could not be older that seventy (young enough to recoup losses). This information was initially gathered by the cold callers, then confirmed by the account opener while completing the paperwork.

When they opened an account, all new clients received several documents and letters, again to protect Stratton Oakmont's collective ass. If clients bothered to read it, they would learn what they could expect from their new Stratton Oakmont brokers:

Dear Client,
Please find the enclosed New Account Application form for your review.
If this document accurately reflects your investment objectives and financial condition, please sign where indicted, keep the last copy for your files, and return the remaining copies to us.

In addition to the New Account Application, we have enclosed the following forms for your signature:
( ) Joint Account Agreement
( ) Corporate Account Agreement
( ) Partnership Agreement
( ) Margin Agreement

and/or please supply one of the following:
( ) Trust Agreement
( ) Profit Sharing Plan & Trust
( ) Other

Please do not alter these forms in any way. If any changes are necessary, please include a signed letter stating same.
We greatly appreciate your business and welcome any suggestions that you might have to better serve your financial needs and goals.
Very truly yours,
Stratton Oakmont, Inc.

The first "Dear Client" letter served several purposes. It required clients to confirm that the numbers given on the account forms accurately reflected their financial conditions, meaning that they were suitable for the proposed type of speculation. That meant, in theory, that clients could not come back later and claim that they could not afford such losses, although they all did anyway. The clients were also confirming that their investment objectives for the account were growth and speculation. Brokers at Stratton Oakmont opening new accounts *always* asked the clients to confirm that: "We're looking for growth and speculation, correct?" The accounts were not allowed to have any other objectives. Most clients barely noticed what the brokers were saying, and if they did, it's doubtful that they realized the importance of the statement. No one ever argued at that point. It was all in the way that it was said.

Frankie always told us that when clients send strangers money over the phone, it was money that they *never* expected to see again. It was their gambling money. I suppose that was how he rationalized stealing their money.

The second "Dear Client" letter spelled out the scam that clients were about to get involved in and apparently was never read closely by new customers.

Dear Client,

Thank you for opening an account with our firm. As an introduction, your initial transaction is usually in a security listed on the NYSE or a Regional Exchange that we are currently recommending.

As we build a relationship, we will usually recommend a security considered speculative in nature that may involve a high degree of risk as well as a high degree of reward. These securities trade in the OTC market listed on the NMS or NASDAQ System and are usually quoted in the *Wall Street Journal.*

Prior to making an investment decision with respect to the purchase of Speculative Growth Securities, prospective investors should carefully consider their investment objectives and their personal financial conditions and should not purchase these securities unless they are able to assume such risk while pursuing potential reward.

Stratton Oakmont, Inc., may be the Investment Banker and a dominant market maker in these securities and may be responsible for a large percentage of the average daily volume. As the dominant market maker, the price of the security may trade at a premium. Additionally, at times these securities may be less liquid, and the ability to sell a large position may depend on the ability of Stratton Oakmont, Inc., to find a buyer.

At any given time, Stratton Oakmont, Inc., may be the only firm writing a research report and recommending the security. We will be glad to provide you with written information from our files (which usually consist of annual reports, news

releases, and the like) concerning any company whose securities you have purchased through your account with us, on request.
Very truly yours,
Stratton Oakmont, Inc.

This letter amazed me. Some would call Stratton Oakmont a bait-and-switch operation, but the letter made it clear from the beginning of the client relationships what was going to happen to them. It essentially warned clients that the first trade was going to be the one and only legitimate stock that they would buy. The second, third, and fourth trades—depending on how long the client hung on—would all be speculative garbage about which they would never be given any type of reliable, unbiased information because they were not covered by any real firm. Clients could count on the stock being totally manipulated since Stratton dominated the market for that stock and was responsible for most of the volume. And to add insult to injury, clients were buying stock in a roach motel (the money went in, but it never came out). It seemed incredible that anyone would open an account knowing such information, which supported my theory that no one ever read it. Either that or they were the sort of compulsive gamblers who know the odds of winning a major lottery, but still think their tickets will hold the winning numbers.

I was amazed to learn what kind of people opened an account with Stratton Oakmont. *Every* kind—as long as they had money: owners of small businesses, large businesses, and every size in between; doctors, lawyers, and probably Indian chiefs. John Albers, the CEO of Dr Pepper, had an account there. The vice president of Dell had an account there. The Pritsker family did deals there. Senator Al D'Amato had an account there. It was unbelievable. Stratton Oakmont brokers were killer salespeople. *Buy or die!*

My favorite customer story at Stratton Oakmont was the Al D'Amato story. The story was kicked around the media shortly after I started working there. Al D'Amato, a state senator in New York, was somehow related to one of the brokers at Stratton and had been convinced to open an account. One of the first stocks he bought was an IPO, Computer Marketplace. He tripled his money in one day! The press had a field day with his success, since good old Al had been shooting his mouth off about the windfall made in the commodities market by a well-known but totally inexperienced investor, Hillary Clinton, who was First Lady at the time. *What about you, Al?* Rookies were not told, though they learned soon enough, that only the privileged, like good old Al, were allowed to sell and realize profits. The rest of the suckers were stuck in the roach motel; they never got out.

Unfortunately, the effect that the story had on me was to make me more defensive of Stratton Oakmont. I would never work in a firm that I thought was literally stealing money. I agreed with the owners that the media was obviously out to get Stratton Oakmont.

"When you're on top, everyone's lookin' to take you down," shouted Frankie. "We're the best. We're *bad*. We're Stratton fuckin' Oakmont!"

Clearly the media had a grudge against Stratton Oakmont, probably because we made too much money. Why else would they write such unfair articles, over and over again? Of course, it made great copy. People loved to read about scandals in the market, insider trading, Michael Milkin, that sort of thing. No one liked to read about a successful start-up firm that raises money for new business, makes money for its clients, and whose employees are extremely well paid and happy. Why else would they write about Al tripling his money, yet fail to mention that *everyone* who bought the stock that day also tripled their money? It took me a year to learn that very few clients ever tripled their money, except occasionally on paper. It wasn't a profit until they could put the money in their pockets, and that wasn't how the firm worked. Clients wanted to collect their money? Not at Stratton Oakmont.

For six months, I worked as an account opener for the Bott. I was wildly successful. There were many perks working for the Bott. The training was tremendous. The Bott had a killer team of account openers: John, Jose, Scott, Michael, and me. John and Scott helped me as often as possible. They knew all the rebuttals.

New accounts were a big deal: the average client at Stratton Oakmont lasted three months. The brokers that worked there accepted that as normal, since that was all they had ever known. I'll never forget the rush I felt when I opened my first account. I had thought that getting my name on the cold caller board in the back of the room felt good, but that was nothing to the thrill of seeing my name up on the whiteboard at the front of the room. At the end of the day, Frankie reviewed the number of accounts opened. Those were the most unbelievable motivational meetings. Anyone who opened an account got applause. When someone got a deuce, that was huge! And for those rare performers who scored a hat trick, as I did on a regular basis, there was crazy wild applause. It felt good to get applause. Maybe that was my fifteen minutes of fame?

I wish I had fully appreciated how great it was working for the Bott and not been in such a hurry to go "out on my own"—that is, sell directly to buyers. Account openers earned three hundred and fifty dollars per week, plus health benefits, and received 15 percent of whatever gross the broker made on the first two trades of any new account. The more accounts I opened for the Bott, the more valuable I became to his group. But the program at Stratton Oakmont was designed to get brokers out on their own as soon as possible. They wanted more of us selling. The deal was that you could go out on your own once you opened twenty accounts. I easily met my goal of opening twenty accounts and securing two hundred fresh leads by September.

The Bott pulled me aside. "Ginger, honey. I know that it looks exciting and glamorous to go on your own. But why not stay with me a little longer? Do you really want to be dealing with those nasty customers by yourself? Buyers are liars!" he was practically begging. "You're not ready to deal with that, and why would you want to? I'll raise your pay a thousand dollars a week. You can continue to add to your lead base. What d'ya say?"

"Uh…okay."

I really didn't have to give it a moment's thought. I could have gone out on my own and survived, but I knew I wasn't fully ready, so it was a no-brainer when the Bott offered me that chance to stay in his group for a base pay more than twice what I had been earning. In the group, after I opened an account for the Bott, that ended my relationship with the customer. I could fall back on the account-openers' disclaimer: "If the customer complains—not my problem. If the customer doesn't pay—not my problem. If the customer doesn't trade—not my problem." Why didn't I realize how great that was?

When I thought back later on the days that I worked for the Bott, I really wondered why I had ever left. But I know why. In those days, for me, it was all about the money. As the Bott would say, "It's a beautiful thing!"

I was hungry to make money. Not a thousand per week; I had made that in the Garment Center. I wanted the *big bucks*. I wanted to be like May Steiner, one of the female brokers at Stratton Oakmont who was making serious money.

May was a young Jewish girl with a sewer mouth. Her customers owned construction companies or sold used cars; they were all tough guys who wanted a broker who was equally tough. Hello, May Steiner!

Smack in the middle of an afternoon meeting, Frankie paused and asked May, "When you go on a date with someone new, do you tell the guy that you make fifty thousand dollars a month?"

"Fuck no! Are you crazy?" May shot back. "Why the fuck would I do that?" The room exploded in laughter. May was all of twenty-three.

If she could do it, so could I. The pressure was on.

When I opened a new account, it had to be signed by a principal of the firm, meaning Josh Shamus or Glen Polansky. Every day they said the same thing to me. "Great job, Ginger. When are you going on your own?"

I always replied, "Soon." I was beginning to realize that they hated the Bott, and hated that he had yet another superstar in his group.

Other brokers asked, too. "Ginger, when are you going on your own?"

The money was clearly there for the taking, and I still hadn't realized that that was exactly what we were doing: *taking* other people's money. But I had my plan, and I stuck with it. Build up a lead base of at least two hundred fresh leads, and then go for it. I was getting better every day at opening accounts.

John, who was also on the Bott's team, looked at me one day and said, "Ginger, you're scaring me." I was that good. I was so good, in fact, that I was sure that John would never live down the day that he threw a lead at me, saying, "You call this fucking guy. He doesn't even speak English!"

"Okay," I said. It was true that the guy had a heavy Chinese accent and wasn't fluent, but he definitely spoke English. Within fifteen minutes, I had the account opened and he was ready to buy stock.

We're bad. We're Stratton fuckin' Oakmont.

I was good. The Bott knew it, and he really wanted to hang on to me as long as possible. He tried hard to keep me happy, and threw me hundred dollar bills like it was nothing. I knew that he was truly desperate when he said, "Ginger, will you marry me? That way you can always be my account opener!"

Oh, how romantic. Even though I *adored* the Bott as my boss, the thought of sleeping with him was too much to take seriously. Fortunately, I knew he was kidding— we were both married. In spite of that, my gut reaction was total repulsion.

"I'd rather die!" I didn't mean for it to come out sounding so cruel but he was by no means my dreamboat. The thought of bedding down that fatty almost made me puke! He was also a typical Long Island Jewish guy, with his entire sense of self-worth centered on his net worth. He was so stunned by my comment that his response was both hilarious and pathetic.

He didn't try to convince me that he was handsome, although if I looked past the weight, he wasn't a bad-looking guy. He didn't try to persuade me that he was brilliant, funny, a good lover, or a good husband, all qualities that a woman might desire in a man. "B-B-But Ginger…I'm a *millionaire!*" the Bott finally spit it out.

I looked back at him evenly. "I'd rather make it on my own." What can I say? I've always been so damn independent.

My independent nature typically was a good thing. I always questioned and challenged my environment. At Stratton Oakmont, I was beginning to have too many unanswered questions. I had begun to suspect that the Jewish mafia was not running a kosher brokerage. I wasn't sure exactly *what* they were doing, but something wasn't right. The rah-rah meetings were totally out of control. The beat-up meetings were unbearable. They were terrifying. I pitied the brokers with desks near the front of the room, or down the center aisle. During the meetings, Frankie walked around the room abusing anyone who happened to be in his view.

"You're nothing but a bunch of lazy piker midget assholes! You make me sick!" When Frankie really lost it, he would grab whatever was close by and throw it—books, papers, Quotrons, it didn't matter. It was an expensive method of making his point, but seeing a three-thousand-dollar computer smash in front of us certainly had an effect. Generally, after one of Frankie's major temper tantrums, we were so scared that we got off our asses and worked like dogs.

The next meeting that Frankie gave would be one of his crazy rah-rah meetings. "You guys are the best! I love you guys! We had an *unbelievable* day! There are nothing but great things happening here. You have absolutely no idea."

We were persuaded that if we left Stratton, we would never be allowed back. We would be out of the family. We would be total failures, doomed to get jobs at McDonalds. One day people would say of us, "You worked at Stratton

Oakmont in the '90s and didn't make any money? Are you fuckin' kidding me? What a loser!"

Frankie would get wildly dramatic to prove his points.

"Michael Milken, in his prime, was making $30 million a year. You guys have an unbelievable opportunity to make money this year, with companies like Octagon Engineering, that went from seven bucks a share to twenty-one in the first day of trading. What would you do if you made thirty million dollars this year?"

We were speechless. Thirty million dollars? I couldn't even imagine that much money. I don't think any of the new brokers could. Frankie loved it. He worked the room. He grabbed his mike and ran to the back of the room where the cold callers sat.

"What would *you* do with thirty million dollars?" He sounded like a game show host.

The young black dude, a brand new cold caller, was the perfect game show contestant. He grinned. "I'd buy me a Cadillac!"

The room exploded in wild hoots and hollers. It didn't matter that yesterday we were assholes. Today we were the best! No one raised money like the brokers at Stratton Oakmont.

The firm had a parking lot that was a sea of luxury cars—Porsches, Ferraris, Beamers, the works—so it made sense that everyone in the room went out of control when they heard Frankie's next round of hyperbole. "You guys have *no idea* what's going to happen at Stratton in the next few years! We're going to take this firm to the next level! The guys that are part of the family will be rich! The guys that are loyal will have opportunities to run firms like Biltmore and Monroe Parker. I want you guys to have it all—hot cars, Rolex watches, houses in the Hamptons. This summer, I want you guys to have so much money that you'll be the biggest assholes in the Hamptons. Just work hard, play hard. Work hard, play hard!"

One of the reasons that I loved working at Stratton was because it could be so much fun. We never knew what to expect. When our stocks ran, we couldn't buy them fast enough. When they crashed, they fell so fast that even if we could sell them, we would not be able to sell them fast enough. It was the most intense environment in which I'd ever I've ever worked. We would go in an instant from manic highs to abysmal lows. The burnout rate was substantial.

Frankie obviously knew this, so when business was good, he invented unique ways of entertaining us.

Since the average Stratton Oakmont broker was a twenty-five-year-old, ball-scratching, macho guy, he needed entertainment of an extreme nature. That led to some wild meetings. It meant drugs, midgets, hookers, and sex. In some firms, two tough guys vying for a top-dog position might consider solving their differences with an arm-wrestling contest outside the office, possibly over drinks at the bar, some Friday night after work. We did that at Stratton Oakmont, but of course we did it in the boardroom, and always in a big way.

Take Neo and Tony. I don't know what or who initiated the challenge, but the gauntlet was tossed. Neo was a compact and extremely well-built Greek god—young, very good looking, and ooh baby, what a body! Rumor has it that the phrase six-pack—the abs, not the beer packaging—had to be coined just for his stomach. He was surely ripped.

Tony was the typical Brooklyn born Guido. An average-looking tough guy who was developing a middle-age paunch already at age twenty-seven, he had a receding hairline and an ego even bigger than his mouth. Although Tony was taller and looked as though he had lifted a weight or two in his day, Neo was solid muscle. I thought that Tony had a chance of winning, but decided to go with team Neo.

The challenge was made, bets were taken, the date was set. All brokers seem to be degenerate gamblers at heart. At least Stratton Oakmont brokers. When I say that bets were made, I'm talking about *big* bets. Thousands of dollars. Frankie would always throw cash into any pot to make it even more appealing. In this bout, the winner would get ten thousand dollars. Even the loser would get several thousand.

On the day of the match, I was surprised to see that someone had rented and carried into the boardroom a professional arm-wrestling stand! I didn't even know that there *were* professional arm-wrestling stands. The table had solid steel legs that were detachable to make it easily transportable. There were pads that covered the top of the table made of high-density foam to create a firm pad for the wrestlers' elbows. We were told that it was an official size and a professional quality table, and it did look formidable. There was no doubt in my mind that it would hold up to even the toughest competition. The stand was high enough so that the wrestlers were able to rest their elbows on the pad from a standing position.

After the market closed for the day, the match was called. I was sure that team Neo was the way to go. My money was on Neo, mostly because he was younger, looked stronger, and was *hot*, but also because I had seen Tony arm-wrestle. He cheated, big time. After the table was set up, the brokers surrounded it, jostling for a good view. I had two grand riding on Neo.

Tony's fans took their place behind him on the right side of the table; Neo's fans stood on the left. Brokers were standing on desks, shouting, laughing, going wild. Neo stripped off his heavily starched white shirt and pumped his pecs. The women in the room gasped. I thought that I would faint. Tony paced in front of his desk, cheered on by his fans.

Finally, the two rivals took their places. The competitors' shoulders needed to be squared to the table before the match could commence, and needed to be a fist's distance away from their hands at the start.

"Ready...set...go!"

The match began. To win in arm-wrestling, of course, one competitor has to force the other's hand down until it makes contact with the table or, in this case, the touch pad. Although it's often just a spur-of-the-moment, un-refereed contest between friends, when it's done competitively it has a number of additional rules, along with fouls and restarts called for various violations. But the last and most important rule of arm-wrestling was this: "Never stop competing until the referee grabs the hands in the center to signify the end of the match."

If there was one good rule for brokers, it would be the same: *Never stop competing!*

Tony quickly took the advantage, and Neo went down. Just as quickly, the match was disallowed—Tony had lifted his elbow off the pad, violating rule number eleven—and set up for restart. The match began again. The screaming and laughing escalated out of control. Neo was grunting and groaning. Tony was sweating profusely. Finally Neo was announced as the winner. Tony was not a happy camper. Men are so competitive.

Just like the arm-wrestling contest, the typical Stratton Oakmont broker considered everything to be a competition. If one broker opened an account, the next had to open two. If one bought ten thousand shares of stock, the next had to buy twenty thousand. The firm purposely promoted that mentality. The whiteboards, the meetings, the public announcement of everyone's gross—it all helped develop competitive, hungry brokers that would make it. Very few women lasted as brokers at Stratton Oakmont, and I could understand why. The brokers were mostly young men, but it was a good ol' boys' club, a macho atmosphere where women were merely tolerated and only begrudgingly allowed into the clubhouse. The brokers considered it totally acceptable to stand in front of the room scratching, grabbing, and adjusting their balls—the male brokers, that is—while giving a meeting.

I tried to picture it in some other corporate environment. It certainly would not have happened at The Right Bank. I couldn't see the average CEO of a *Fortune* 500 company standing up at an annual meeting with his hand on his crotch.

I asked my husband Freddy. "Honey, when you go to a meeting at AIG, do the men grab their balls?"

"What the hell are you talking about, Ginger?"

"Well, I was just wondering if any of the men there, when they get nervous or whatever...do they grab their balls, adjust themselves, you know...?"

"No! Are you crazy?"

"I just wondered. You know, I spent twenty years working in the Garment Center, and I never saw anyone do that, even though garmentos can be a little strange," I said. "But I though maybe they were the exception, and maybe this ball-grabbing activity became acceptable in corporate America and I missed it. It is just so accepted at Stratton Oakmont."

Freddy looked at me like I was mentally disturbed.

"There is not a vice president or manager or lowly worker that would *ever* stand the front of a room and grab his balls. It just wouldn't happen."

"That's reassuring," I said. "The only other men I've ever seen so blasé about crotch grabbing are baseball players and musicians."

I laughed, but in truth, I found it somewhat troubling. Not because I was a prude—I was far from that—but because it was just so typical of the whole male chauvinist, macho superiority crap that I had to wade through every day at Stratton Oakmont. There were women who worked there, but we were treated as either insignificant, invisible, or, if we played along, as one of the guys. The men talked openly about women as though they were nothing more than possessions or conquests, beings that existed for the brokers' pleasure. Very few of the guys were married, or I should say, few admitted to being married. They loved nothing more than loudly sharing conversations detailing the most intimate moments with some jerk's latest girlfriend, one-nighter, or hooker.

The brokers considered it cool to hire hookers. If they had the money to pay for it, they must be big brokers, right? That's what it was all about: who had the nicest car, the baddest watch, the hottest bitch, the highest tickets, the biggest dick. Most brokers at Stratton Oakmont did not give a shit about anything *real*. They would never survive there if they did.

Maybe Frankie's philosophy was right: Just buy stock. If it goes up, buy more. If it goes down, buy more. It doesn't matter. Do not care; just buy stock. The macho, competitive atmosphere helped us survive, in that sense; Frankie always told us that if we cared, we would never be successful brokers. We would never make money. We would never be *rich*. He was right. The biggest mistake that a broker could make was to do nothing. I supposed that these lectures were designed to prepare us for irate clients when our stocks crashed.

That was the one thing we could count on: the stocks would always crash. When that happened, and clients called, the conversations were fairly predictable. "Ginger, what's my position in Dual Star trading at?"

"Hmmmm, let's see. DSTR is at three and a quarter by four. Things look great! I think you should buy more at this level."

"Are you kidding me? I knew that one was a dog with fleas! You know I bought it at seven. Why would I buy more?"

"Yeah, I know that you're down 50 percent. We are expecting good news on this company. If you can add another twenty thousand shares to your position, it will bring your cost down. Then when the stock spikes up we'll bang out of there and book you a profit of twenty to thirty grand! Let's go with twenty thousand shares. It's a small cash investment of eighty grand. What d'ya say?"

I knew what they would say, or at least what most of them would say. "*You are out of your fucking mind! I would not touch that with a ten-foot pole!*"

But every now and then, someone said, "Do it." And *that* was a beautiful thing.

I thought it was funny, considering my previous career, to think that stocks were the only thing that people were afraid to buy on sale. Clothes, cars, and even houses look better when they are half price. But people look at cheap stocks in a different way.

As an account opener, I didn't have to deal with many problems. I only had to focus on opening accounts. It gave me some protection from the nastiness while I learned more about the rest of the business. When the Bott taught us that "buyers are liars," he spoke from experience. I thought he was kidding until I had my own clients.

In the Series 7 material, we learned that settlements on stock trades take place in five business days. Of course that was in the '90s; it is now three days. Anyone who didn't pay for a trade was considered to be free riding. That was illegal, yet there were almost no consequences for investors who didn't pay. If clients agreed to buy stock but had no equity in their accounts, the brokers assumed the responsibility. Therefore, if the clients never paid and the stock ended up being sold at a loss, the brokers took the hit. If the clients had equity in their account, the brokers could sell enough stock to cover the debit. If not, too bad.

I was always amazed at how many ruthless, free-riding, scumbag clients were out there. Many clients opened accounts knowing that they did not have the money to pay for their trades, intending to take a profit and close out the account if the stock went up by settlement. The two key dates that investors needed to know about were the trade date, which is the date the order was placed, and the settlement date, which was the time the transfer of shares was completed and payment was due. When I first started in the industry, settlement took seven days, then five, and later three, where remained as of 2013. In the 1990s, most clients paid by sending in personal checks via snail mail. Electronic transfer? There was really no such thing for individuals at the time.

Likewise, few individuals had access to the Internet, and the World Wide Web was still just a in its infancy, fresh off Tim Berners-Lee's drawing board. I had heard something about it, but I wasn't sure what it was. I will always remember Vito, another broker at Stratton Oakmont, telling me about the Internet.

"All the college campuses are talking about it. The Internet is the hottest thing ever!"

"Okay, okay. But what *is* it?" I asked him.

"It's the World Wide Web, *man!*"

5

THE PARTY

AFTER I HAD worked at Stratton Oakmont for almost a year, I received an invitation in the mail. It was an invitation for me and my husband, Freddy, to attend the Stratton Oakmont Christmas party. Sal asked me if I was going.

"Well, of course we're going. We love to dance and we love to party!" I was excited, but I had no idea what to expect. The party was going to be held at the Water's Edge in Long Island City. Since I'd never been there, I wasn't sure what we'd find. In 1994, Long Island City was filled with old warehouses, and was not an area that most people would want to frequent. Anyone going somewhere in Long Island City was probably looking for trouble, sex, or drugs.

Of course, most brokers at Stratton Oakmont, including me, were looking for all three!

I was so excited to be included. I even had the perfect dress. I told Amy, "I bought a designer sample when I was working in the Garment Center that I want to wear. It's a black watch plaid—so *holiday*—done in chiffon. It's strapless and poufed—absolutely beautiful."

Amy was half listening. She mumbled, "Yeah, that sounds like it might work for someone your age."

Thank God when I put it on that night it didn't fit. Not that it wasn't beautiful—it was. But it was dated, and it would have dated me. Plus, I had lost so much weight that it would have fallen off me. I decided to go with a tight black Sue Wong mini with bejeweled décolletage. It was perfect.

Sal had offered to pick up Freddy and me in his limo, which really worked out great. I had learned from others at the company that Stratton Oakmont parties were like limo parking lots. Even though most brokers personally drove Porsches or Ferraris to work, no one would just *drive* to the party. Driving themselves would most likely get them tagged as a piker midget asshole.

My intel had been right. When Freddy and I arrived at the Water's Edge, we looked around and did not see one car—although we were not exactly reliable sources of information that night since we werea all totally wasted even before the party officially started—but the road leading to the entrance of the Water's Edge did look like a sea of limos.

I was feeling no pain that night and I looked marvelous. The night started when Sal and his wife, Debbie, pulled up at our house with the limo, along with another broker, Alan Perez, and his girlfriend, Sue.

"Wow, Ginger. You look so hot! I can't believe you are the same person that I work with! This is Deb."

"Hey, Debbie," I said, smiling. "Nice to meet you. Sal has told me everything there is to know about you, and then some."

"It isn't true."

"What? What isn't true?"

"Anything he told you! None of it is true."

Sal just smiled. He said, "You know Alan, of course. This is Sue."

"Nice to meet you, Ginger."

"Everyone? This is my husband, Freddy."

"So, I finally meet the gang," said Freddy. "I sincerely want to thank you both for putting up with my wife. You guys see her more than I do. I don't know how you do it!"

Sal looked at Freddy, then shook his head. "It ain't easy, dude."

"Are you guys ready to rock?" I asked. "Let's get this party started!" I invited them to sit in the living room. Our tiny house in Port Washington was almost a classic Dutch Colonial, though we had updated it with a front portico and eyelash window. We'd painted the interior in antique white with pure white accents.

"Wow! What a nice home you have," Debbie said, as we settled into the living room.

I laughed. "We bought some of our furniture in Vermont. This was the only sofa that we could agree on, so we drove up there, loaded it into the van, and turned right around and came home." We had both fallen in love with the sofa, which was a fairly classic two-cushion style with rolled arms, updated with a clever mix of fabrics and finished off with antique gold studs strategically placed around the cushions.

Freddy broke out a bottle of our favorite champagne, Moët & Chandon— pretty decadent, considering that I had not yet started making the big bucks I was eagerly anticipating, and we were behind on every bill. "Have you guys ever done champagne shooters?"

I put out three pairs of crystal shot glasses. "This is our favorite way to drink champagne. It's as if we're doing shots. It tastes good, and then it hits you."

We drank a few rounds. Freddy offered to make drinks, pour wine, and crack open beers, but I felt that something was lacking. "Freddy, I feel like that's not enough for this special occasion," I said. "It's time to take our heads to the next level."

I went over to the corner of the living room to the antique oak secretary that I had inherited from my uncle. I opened a small hidden drawer and took out the clear plastic bag, along with a beautiful pewter-encased mirror. The bag contained pure white powder.

"Uncut cocaine. Freddy, may I have a bill and a blade, please?"

Freddy opened a drawer in the coffee table and took out a straight-edge razor blade. He reached into his wallet and grabbed a hundred-dollar bill. Perfect. After everyone did a few lines, it was time to leave if we wanted to get there fashionably late, but not so late that we missed all the fun. We were all pretty wasted, so I was really grateful for Sal's limo driver.

We packed up our mirror and climbed into the back seat of Sal's limo, which was parked in the driveway. It was a short ride to the Water's Edge, and at that hour there wouldn't be too much traffic. I looked over at Sal, whose eyes had never looked bluer. He looked so hot in his tux. Sitting next to him in the limo, I was really getting turned on. My dress was so tight and short that I could not help but show almost every inch of my fabulous legs. I could tell that Sal was captivated, and wondered if I should make a move on him.

I loved the combination of champagne and cocaine. There was only one thing that I could think of that would make my head feel even better, and would be fucking Sal in the limo. Fortunately, it occurred to me that since I was there with Freddy, and Sal was there with his wife, maybe getting it on with Sal was not a good idea. I looked at Freddy. He was wasted. I looked at Sal. Completely wasted. What should I do?

Sal's voice suddenly brought me back to reality. "Ginger, do you have a light?" I didn't. "No? Shit. Freddy? Freddy, wake up, damn it! We need matches!"

Freddy looked at me with a confused expression. Then he looked at Sal's hands. "Ah...smoking a doob to top it off. What a great idea!"

"I brought some kick-ass weed," said Sal. We all took several hits until it was gone. The reefer kicked in fast.

We were completely out of control. I could tell that Freddy wanted sex. Badly. His hands were all over me, caressing my neck and breasts, moving up my skirt. *It would be fun in the limo. Really fun. But no, no, please stop, Freddy.* There was not enough time for the orgy that it would have become. I noticed that even Alan looked exceptionally sexy that night. There was something about a guy in a tuxedo that really turned me on. Oh my god.

"Honeybunny? Can we do another line?" I looked at Freddy. He whipped out the mirror, and we snorted away.

I was starting to worry. Long Island City was only twenty minutes from our house, and we were already so wasted. "I really don't think that I can make it inside," I said. "I know that I'll be fine once I get in there, but walking, climbing steps..."

Alan, who had not said a word until now, looked at me. "Come on, Ginger. You can do it. We want to dance! We want to party!"

Freddy held my arm and helped me out. I followed the mink in front of me. In addition to a limo, having a mink coat was apparently another requirement for attendance. For my part, I wore a magnificent $10,000 Blackglama mink, the most incredible mink that I had ever seen! Fashioned in European style, ankle length, it was made with only the best female skins. I looked absolutely amazing in it! I did no give a rat's ass about PETA! No bullshit organization was going to tell *me* what I could and could not wear!

Anyway, I hated the cold and there was nothing like a mink coat to stay warm.

I was so high that as I had feared, I barely made it through the front door. I remember that it was nice and warm inside. I don't remember if I walked fast or slow. I tried blending into a bunch of minks, but that strategy failed. I felt someone staring at me, and bumped into Glen Polansky, possibly the last person I wanted to see. I kept going. Maybe he hadn't seen me after all? No chance of that. Glen was making a beeline for me. There was no way to avoid him now!

When Glen saw me that night, I could tell that he was stunned by how beautiful I looked. I didn't get it. Did everyone think I was a former librarian? He had never really acted as though he noticed me before, in that way, at least that I knew. In the office, I did dress rather more like a schoolteacher than I had for the party. I couldn't imagine him somehow "doing" an account opener, but that night I looked different. I felt as thought there was something about me that night that was irresistible.

Glen grabbed me and kissed me hello. Why had he done that? My knees were so weak, they almost buckled. "Ginger, You look incredible!"

Shit! He remembered my name. How was that possible? I looked at Glen Polansky. I had never seen a man who looked so hot in a tuxedo! Glen was exactly the type of guy that I had always been looking for, all my life. Our eyes met, just for a second, and we both knew that the "conversation" would be continued—maybe not that night, but sometime in the near future.

I have no idea what I said to Glen, but it didn't really matter. I had to have him. I *would* have him.

I found my way back to Freddy. Our group had grabbed a table near the dance floor. Wonderful. It finally gave me a chance to take in the surroundings.

Holy shit! This was Wall Street at its most decadent. Greed *is* good!

That was the first time that I had ever seen Freddy speechless. Freddy was working on Wall Street for AIG at the time and had thought nothing of being invited to yet another black-tie affair. They were pretty standard stuff. But even he had not been to an opulent affair like Stratton Oakmont's party. Since the Water's Edge was not in Manhattan, but across the river, it offered a breathtaking view of midtown Manhattan. If I had been there for an ordinary dinner, it would have been difficult to notice anything other than that scene-stealing view. But the Stratton Oakmont Christmas party was not an ordinary normal dinner.

I thought back to that Christmas party in the late 70's at the World Trade Center when I worked at The Right Bank—the party were Bill Levine had parted ways after the incredible limo ride. Though the Twin Towers had offered an amazing view, too, but I had hardly noticed it that night. My thoughts were only of Bill and that was what captivated me. The party was held in one of the four banquet halls located within the Trade Center on the top floors of the North Tower. In addition to Windows on the World, a smaller restaurant called Wild Blue, and a bar called The Greatest Bar on Earth, there were several rooms for private functions. Together they equaled fifty thousand square feet of space.

The room that hosted The Right Bank's party was a traditional banquet hall. They had your usual linen-covered tables accented with floral arrangements that would be standard in any banquet hall. The color scheme and décor was very 1970s, with earth-toned linens, plush rust-colored chairs, and a rust-and-white plaid rug. In spite of the unfortunate color scheme, the room maintained an upscale look and appeal because of that spectacular view. The view was clearly the focal point of the room, with floor-to-ceiling windows that wrapped the building. The view showed the entire southern tip of Manhattan, but I had been too busy looking for Bill Levine to notice. Bill had been the object of my desirous thoughts in those days, as I believed I had been the object of his. Where was Bill? I was so focused on his arrival that I barely noticed the festive Holiday decorations in the room or the long list of guests that attended this party. As head designer for The Right Bank, I knew that it was important for me to make the rounds that night, to chat with the salespeople and talk a big game, but I could not focus. All I could think about that night, as I absent-mindedly drank one glass of wine after another, was whether he was ever going to show up to his own party. Was he a no-show?

"Ginger, can you believe this party?" Freddy's voice brought me back to present-day reality.

When Stratton Oakmont did something, it always did it in a big way. The firm had reserved two floors of the banquet hall, as well as space on a riverboat that was docked on one side of the restaurant. The first floor was for drinking and dancing, and had an amazing sound system presided over by a DJ who rocked the house. The second floor was for dining, although it also featured an incredible ten-piece band.

Neither Freddy nor I had ever seen a buffet spread so massive and all-encompassing. Although as a rule I really disliked buffets that one impressed me-as though anyone could fail to be impressed by food that was framed against the unbelievable backdrop of the Manhattan skyline. They didn't just have salad, they had three huge bowls of crisp, dark green Romaine lettuce that were quickly replaced the moment they looked limp or were getting low. There wasn't just fish: there was a tremendous table of huge dishes, each filled to the top with all a variety of seafood: clams, lobster, and calamari. They had piles and piles of plump pink shrimp, and perhaps the most incredible assortment of sushi outside of Japan—an entire table covered with it! For meat lovers, they had a carving station serving melt-in-your-mouth, paper-thin slices of filet mignon. There were tables of breads and starches, side dishes, fruits and vegetables, and, of course, desserts.

The irony was that we were so coked up that we could not eat!

"Who cares about food? All I want to do is dance. Come on, Freddy. Let's party."

We danced for what seemed like hours, but wasn't, then decided to explore the riverboat. The riverboat provided a quiet escape for the folks, like Frankie's dad, who wanted to have a conversation, to shoot the shit and actually hear what was said. Frankie had invited both of his parents to the party. Jared's dad was there, as well as an assortment of aunts and uncles adding their small part to the thousand-odd merrymakers who had descended on the Water's Edge that night. The New Orleans jazz band was a great touch. The room where they played was draped and bedazzled in its holiday finest. The glowing bulbs on the magnificent Christmas tree, like with the sparkling lights of Manhattan, were mirrored in merry, dancing reflections by the river. The party planners thought of everything: white-glove service, elegant trimmings, delightful amenities. The place had it all.

All of the rooms Stratton Oakmont had reserved were packed with hundreds of beautiful ladies and handsome men. Freddy could not stop grinning—he loved pretty ladies, and the party certainly had plenty of them. They came in droves: short ones, tall ones, black ones, white ones. The only thing that they seemed to have in common was that they were all beautiful.

In spite of, or because of, the fact that no one was worried about being politically correct, it was an amazing Christmas party. It was unimportant that the owners of Stratton Oakmont were Jewish garmentos. Only about 10 percent of the employees were Jewish, so they called it a Christmas party. Come on! How bad could those guys be?

Frankie gave one of his least memorable speeches ever that night, although in fairness few people really wanted to listen to him talk that night or were any shape to follow it or remember it later. I do recall that he said Merry Christmas. I may have been the only person who heard this, but I am certain that he said it. He threw in a Happy Chanukah or two, but that was understandable since his dad was there.

Everyone who was anyone connected to Stratton Oakmont was at the party. Jared Bellmore, the founder of the firm was there. I had always thought of him as just a skinny short Jewish schmuck from Queens, but he really cleaned up well! He looked so hot in his obviously custom-made tuxedo that it just took my breath away. Maybe it was the champagne or the coke or the pot or the combination of all three, but looking at him I suddenly found it so unbearably hot in that room that I had the incredible urge to get completely naked. I would not have thrown Jared Bellmore out of bed for eating crackers.

I looked over at Freddy, and I swear to this day that I saw him drooling. I was so wasted that night that I had barely noticed that we were with the most beautiful group of people that I had ever seen. I never heard exactly how many people actually attended the party that night, but Frankie mentioned that a thousand people had RSVP'd that they would attend. And Freddy was checking them all out. He kept babbling something about the guys at work not believing that he went to a party with what seemed like five hundred models in spectacular dresses, many of which probably cost more than my car. Freddy did tell me that he suspected that many of the women at the party had been *hired* to attend, and given the brokers' penchant for hookers, that would not be surprising. He asked me why I thought the brokers were so interested in hookers given that so many of the wives were beautiful.

"We're surrounded by young, good-looking, wealthy brokers. They're all big shots with cash, and they like to throw their money around. Those types are magnets for a certain type of incredibly gorgeous ladies," I said. "They all have them. Look at the Bott, look at Jared, look at Frankie. Their wives are beautiful. The Bott's wife is a blond beauty, Jared's wife—AKA The Duchess of Bay Ridge—is breathtaking. Even Glen has a pretty wife. Although I hear that she's an unbelievable bitch. You know, just show the money and the ladies will follow."

Freddy was not convinced.

"Well, I guess you're right. But I still think that half the women in this room are hookers. They are just too pretty."

I had a feeling that tonight, no one looking for romance would be disappointed. It was the most outrageous Christmas party that I had ever been to, and the setting was romantic. Words could not describe the magical Christmas décor that enveloped this world-class restaurant and set the tone for the night. If greed was good, then this was fucking great! There was nothing left out. Nothing. I was happy that we had arrived early enough to be able to appreciate how incredible the place was. I had always loved poinsettias, and there were hundreds, possibly thousands of them in all different colors (red, white, pink, and even yellow-white). They were beautiful beyond belief.

The tables were impeccably covered in a festive Christmas-red linen, accented with beautiful but simple centerpieces. They were large enough to grab your attention but small enough so as not to interfere with conversations. Not that there was much talking going on: I had no fear of a co-worker initiating a conversation because most of the people in the room were just as wasted as we were, if not worse! And we were *so* wasted that all we wanted to do, all we *could* do, was dance.

I turned to Freddy and gave him the look. "Let's go, baby. Get up off your ass. You know what I want. All I want to do is dance!" I was just an average dancer, but Freddy always stole the show. He was beautiful to watch, so graceful that he always made me look good. It was hard to believe that Fred was a total klutz in many other ways. At one point, we were the only couple on the dance floor. After about five minutes, Glen got up to dance with his wife.

I decided that night that Glen was the man of my dreams. Only for sex of course, he was not the relationship type. I could picture him naked, and knew he would be hot in bed. I was determined to see for myself and find out for sure. Not that night, of course, since I was with Freddy and I truly loved him. But I was determined, and I set my sights on Glen Polansky.

Freddy and I had been on the dance floor when the Bott arrived. I thought it strange even after we were seated he hadn't come over to wish us Merry Christmas, but he was so surrounded by ass-kissers that it would have been hard for him to break away. It was really unbelievable! Freddy noticed what was going on with the Bott and asked me if he had a ring to kiss, like the pope. I laughed. Just like the pope, the Bott was holding an audience. The Bott was the man!

I was afraid that in my altered state, I might humiliate myself if I talked to the Bott. Anyway, I wanted to dance some more, so I grabbed my man. As we started to leave for the disco room, I realized that Frankie was calling a meeting. I couldn't believe it! What? Was he kidding? How could he possibly hope to capture the room's attention in this environment? He gave a brief speech about the year, how amazing it had been, and named the brokers who had made more than a million dollars in commissions. He talked a little about what we could look forward to next year.

"We have an unbelievable calendar of deals to do. I think we had a lot of fun with the deals that we took public. We saw some big performers. We had, last year, we had twenty-five guys—no, people, because there were some women in there—who did over a million dollars in commissions. I expect that list to grow dramatically, and I want that list to grow. There are a lot of people in this room that should do it next year," he said. Personally, I hoped I would be one of them, and I planned to try. "I think that we crossed the line from a brokerage firm to an institution, and I want everybody to be here for the long term. We've told everybody in the community that (a) We're here for the long term; (b) We're doing more business than most other firms; and (3) Next year—HEY, EVERYONE, LISTEN UP! I AM TALKING ABOUT NEXT YEAR—What we're gonna do next year is *tear down the house*. This will be the year for the young people who want to jump in, get involved, raise money. I'm waiting for the young guys to step up. THIS IS YOUR YEAR! God bless America, and God bless Stratton Oakmont."

For once, Frankie did not exactly capture everyone's attention. We were not in the mood for his typical Stratton Oakmont family bullshit—We want to dance! We want to party!—but he ended on a high note with a message for the brokers. "I want to say my six favorite words to the young brokers here: Mo' money…mo' money…mo' money!"

That got our attention!

Glen grabbed the mike from Frankie. "The one person he will not get up and talk about is himself. Without Frankie, none of this would have been possible, so let's give him a round of applause!"

And at that exact moment, the "entertainment" descended on the room. I thought it was tacky, inappropriate, and disgusting, but as usual, the boys ruled at Stratton Oakmont. "If you don't like it, tough shit. Go home!"

The so called "entertainment" consisted of five half-naked women dancing and shaking their flabby asses under the guise of Brazilian dancers in different-colored beaded thong bikinis. The red one was adorned with black beaded fringe on the top that was added for the sole purpose of focusing attention on the dancer's tits. Actually, all the tops had the same tassel-like fringe. The dancers wore feather-trimmed caps that seemed more Vegas than Rio, beaded and encrusted with giant plumes. I could not imagine how they managed to keep their headpieces on while dancing. Several of the dancers finished off their outfits with over-the-elbow-length gloves. So Folies Bergère.

When the girls finished shakin' their stuff, it was the guys' turn. There were two men in tight red-and-white-striped stretch pants that made them seem more like circus stars than dancers. Big deal. They were shirtless, but I was not impressed. No six-packs there. Not great dancers and not even buff bods? Women in business *always* got the short end of the stick! We didn't even get men in thong bikinis. There was nothing that was here for the women. I couldn't even get a feel for the size of their packages, so they must have worn jock straps. In any case, it was such a bizarre display of decadence and so very Boom-Boom Room-like. Only a brokerage firm would have the nerve to provide that type of entertainment at a Christmas party. The women continued to shake their beaded tits and gave us at least ten minutes of butt time. The men seemed to do a pathetic version of a break dance.

Growing up in New York often left people jaded. If people were break-dancing in the street for money, they had to be the best break-dancers ever, or they would starve to death. People would pass them right by without a glance. So, although the show was mildly entertaining, I could only take so much. Come on, Freddy! Let's dance.

But it was not to be. We had to endure one last speaker, Jared Bellmore. Man, he really cleaned up nice. His speech was pathetic—I was so disappointed, because I had heard that he was an incredible motivator and taught Frankie everything—and he had a hard time getting started. There was a lot of shushing.

Shhhhhhhhh.

"No way. We want to party," someone whispered loudly.

Shhhhhhhhh.

"No way. We want to party. We want to *party!*"

It was hard to hear Jared, but I did catch some of his speech. "Everybody, don't worry. I will make this really short—"

Somebody shouted, "Midget! No piker midget assholes allowed!"

"Ahhh, come on! No short jokes!" laughed Jared. "Anyway, this has been a strange year for me. It's the first Christmas party that I've been out of the business. Usually at this party, I thank people who have been instrumental in building our business, our family. The problem is, now I can't name all the people because the list keeps getting bigger and bigger—there are so *many* people instrumental in our success. I just want to say one thing…I look at things right now—"

"Shhhhh!" I heard his dad, Mad Mel, scream out, in his obnoxious way, "Knock it off, goddamn it. Shhhhh!"

Jared continued. "Uh, oh! Don't piss off my father! Anyway, I look at things a bit differently now, ya know, 'cause I'm out of the business…and the one thing I can tell you, the one word that comes to my mind is that I'm *proud*. I have pride in what I accomplished. I think everybody here should have pride that you are part of an amazing organization. Things like this don't happen to most people. This is a once-in-a-lifetime chance, being part of an organization that has such a family-oriented feeling. And integrity. And loyalty. It's a place where people can come to work and feel that they are part of the family. I used to own this firm. Another year, another great Stratton Oakmont Christmas party. I am proud to be here. And I love everybody! It's just a special thing. God bless everybody. Merry Christmas, Happy New Year, Happy Chanukah, Happy Holidays."

He walked over to his dad, who was standing next to Danny's father and Jared said to him:

"This man planted the seed. I love him like he was my father."

Do we really care? But he lost us. *No more speeches tonight. Please spare us! Shhhhhhhhhh.*

"We want to party. We want to *party*!"

"You are all privileged to be part of the Stratton family."

BLAH BLAH BLAH.

Shhhhhhhhhh.

"*We want to party*!"

I do try not to be a rude person, so I did stay until the godfather came back out! That, of course, was Frankie, the mafia don wannabe. He wore a white tuxedo. He kissed Jared when he finished his speech. Who does that, besides Marlon Brando? It was too much.

"Come on, Freddy. Let's dance."

One thing that the fearless Brazilian babes had provided was that they served as a sexual stimulant for the men. I saw Mad Mel dancing with my Nazi friend. Frau Anna Keller. He appeared to be humping her!

Freddy finally looked at me and said, "Okay, let's go!"

We decided to head back to the dance floor. The brief interruption only fueled our fire. I noticed a stairwell in a somewhat remote corner, whipped out my mirror and Freddy simultaneously rolled up a bill. That whole display of flabby flesh had brought our heads down!

"We've only got a little bit left, but it should be enough for the two of us to get high." After we had snorted every last bit of the cocaine, we turned to go, but before we were able to return to the main room, the door flew open and in stormed Glen Polansky. It was not that he was mad, he just had a commanding presence and moved with such intensity that EVERYONE assumed he was mad. *Shit! Why now?* I knew that my nose was covered in white powder. Glen just looked at me and smiled. He did not say a word as he hurried past us.

Freddy and I walked as fast as possible back to the main room. I saw that almost everyone in the disco room was wearing sunglasses. I knew my eyes were so bloodshot that there would be no doubt that I had been up to no good, too, and wished that I had thought to bring my dark shades. Then I looked closer and realized that the glasses were party favors!

"Ohhh, Freddy! I want a pair. Where can we get some?"

"Ginger, Babe. You're on your own. I have no freakin' idea."

"Forget it. Let's dance. I love this song."

The dance floor was packed with people decked out in sunglasses, Hawaiian leis, neon necklace tubes, and several half-moon metallic masks. The masks were quite striking, though I could not decide if they were fabulous or creepy.

At this point, we had been at the Christmas party for several hours. We knew it would not be cool to stay longer. It was time. I decided to visit the ladies room before we left, and I noticed that many of the women were leaving the MEN's room. Judging from the looks on their faces, they had either been getting high or getting laid! Whichever it was, I wanted some of that action.

I was just about to explore what new possibilities lurked in the men's room when I noticed my sweet Freddy, standing there in front of the door, as if on guard duty. Protecting Ginger from this promised garden of earthly delights. Darn.

I want to go in there!

FUCK ME!

"Oh, honey, I thought this was the ladies room."

Glen Polansky happened to be going into the men's room at the time. He and I made eye contact and he winked at me. I got the message. It might not be tonight, or tomorrow night, but it would happen soon! I thought of Bill Levine and remembered his soulful brown eyes. That was the same look that Bill had given me. Without uttering one word, Glen told me everything that I needed to know: "I want you and I know that you want me. But not tonight."

And just like that, we were done, out of there. We collected our coats, hats, and gloves and headed over the river to cruise Manhattan, looking for fun. Someone at the Christmas party had mentioned that many people would be going to the Palladium. So off we went. Anyone who made the club scene, or hit the discos, as we still called them in the '90s, knew that it was extremely important to arrive late. Not fashionably late but really late: one or two o'clock in the morning late. That was the only way to get in. Come in a limo and come late. We were all fired up and ready to take on the Palladium. Sal rolled a doob and passed it around. We couldn't wait!

"We want to dance. We want to party! Pass that doobie! This is really good shit, Sal. Where did you get it?"

"I get my weed from one of the drivers who works for me. The dude has this connection in the hood that is not to be believed!"

The Palladium was a large theater-turned-dance club in New York near Union Square on Fourteenth Street, not the nicest area in town. Opened by Studio 54's Steve Rubell and Ian Schrager, it was every bit as over-the-top and had become *the* place to be seen. Like Studio, as the in crowd referred to Studio 54, the Palladium had a strategy for making clubs desirable to the glitterati: don't let *anyone* in. There were many occasions when we stood outside like dejected brides left at the altar. It was different if you knew someone inside.

Tonight was no different. And so we waited. And we waited. And waited. It was upsetting to see the cast of characters that *was* being allowed in. Who did *they* know? Suddenly, a bus pulled up in front of where we were standing. It was filled to capacity with wasted Stratton Oakmont brokers, who were ushered right in. That was not a simple undertaking: we watched the brokers descend from the bus, and most of them could hardly walk. That they made it inside at all was certainly a testament to their willpower and desire to dance and party.

"Finally! They're going to let us in. I'm so excited!"

"Hey, Ginger, do *not* show it. The bouncers will change their minds!" Alan cautioned me to be cool.

"True. We *bad!* We *Stratton fuckin' Oakmont!*" I whispered to Sal. He started laughing. It was a giggle, really. I caught a case of uncontrollable giggles, and could not even look at Sal. But I kept up my chant.

We *bad!* We *Stratton fuckin' Oakmont!* We want to *party!*

They let us in. We walked down a number of dimly lit stairs and into a sea of flesh on the dance floor. The DJ was out of control, and the crowd loved it, and so did we! We all felt incredible that night. I imagined myself to be a foxy E.T. Freddy was my greasy Latin lover, who had taken me prisoner. Sal and Alan were my man-servants; their wives were my foot- maids. We were smokin' hot on the dance floor. How could we be anything but hot? The dance floor was so crowded that we could barely move. I was happy about that: by three o'clock after hours of partying, I could barely stand, let alone dance. For most of the time that we were at the Palladium, I think Freddy was holding me up. Or was it the crowd?

"Wow! We are hot, baby, hot."

It was the kind of magical night that I wanted to store away in my memory banks to replay over and over again later. Overhead, were these circles that seemed to be rotating in sync with the music. Watching them made me feel insane. E.T. was taking me up to them to another world, to another galaxy.. *Take me now!* It was the *most* unbelievable experience of my life!. Of course, by that point I was so incredibly wasted that I might have felt the same way about some old VFW hall with a jukebox, as long as people were dancing. I looked up into the mezzanine level and saw what looked like thousands of people moving to the beat of the music, dancing on different levels. I had never seen so many people in a single club, and it seemed like Freddy and I, over the years, had danced at every club in New York (with and without each other).

Eventually, even though the crowd was friendly, my claustrophobia kicked in, and the club began to feel unbearably packed. I knew that it was time to go. When I got into the limo, I immediately passed out, and slept the entire ride home wrapped in Freddy's arms. I felt calm and secure. It would be business as usual come Monday morning.

6

TALK A BIG GAME

As an account opener for the Bott, my salary jumped to a thousand a week. The Bott was probably the best boss that I had ever had. He never gave negative feedback, only positive reinforcement. He gave bonuses for doing an exceptional job. And he made working at Stratton Oakmont fun. I would have extended my time with the Bott indefinitely if I had known then what I know now. But I was not happy making a thousand a week. I wanted the *big bucks*. I wanted to make as much as the independent brokers were making. I wanted to go out on my own. I was ready.

Going out on my own...what did that really mean? It meant that I would be in charge of my own book of business. It meant that if customers were unhappy about losing money, I had to deal with them. It meant that I would be the beneficiary of all the hours spent cold calling. In a perfect world, it meant knowing what stocks to buy and when to sell them—although I hadn't yet realized that in the roach motel, we never sold stock. But the most important reason that brokers went on their own at Stratton Oakmont was that it let them keep all the money! I would keep all the money!

Well, not really all of it. Stratton took 50 percent. But I would keep the rest. I liked that math. I decided to go ask en for advice on whether or not I was ready to go on my own, and to do a "Sharon Stone "on him, which meant leaving my panties behind. I waited until Josh left the office that they shared, and decided to go for it. Josh was in with the cold callers giving one of his recycled AA speeches, so I knew that I had at least a good thirty minutes. I wanted him so badly, I could taste it. I could taste him.

I knew it was wrong, but it felt right at the time. My marriage was falling apart. It seemed that Freddy didn't want me anymore. He and I fought constantly, and we almost never had sex anymore. I told myself that having sex with him was the only reason I had married him in the first place .If that was over, then most likely, so was our marriage. I was hardly home to spend time with him, but even when I was, all he wanted to do was sit around watching the creepy shows that he liked, like *Forensic Files*.

I had seen so many episodes of that show that I could recite many of the lines verbatim: "The house was broken into with no visible means of forced entry." That was a favorite. "The orange fibers found in his car were identical to the orange rug that they had in the bedroom." Wouldn't the color be enough? And I could always guess the ending: the husband murdered the wife or the wife murdered the husband. The people usually had such weak alibis! It was obvious that they were not the sharpest tools in the shed. It seemed as though they would be better off admitting that they killed someone rather than trying some pathetic, half-baked alibi.

I told Freddy that I would be like O. J. Simpson. "I'm going to kill you one day, and get off!" Well, we joked about it, but sometimes I felt that watching *Forensic Files* was like watching a training video for my future.

When Freddy and I first got married, we had unbelievable sex. Hot, screaming, mind-blowing sex. I was never the type to refuse my husband with a headache excuse because I wanted it more than he did, *much* more. And I wanted it often. As Freddy's brother Donnie used to say, "You only need to fuck a woman *right* one time. After that, she's yours for life."

True.

What was a girl to do? When that seemed to have ended, or diminished anyway, I needed to find someone else. The easiest target was Glen. He was sexy, willing, and such a hound dog! He was perfect.

I went into Glen's office and asked if I could speak to him for a few minutes, that I needed some advice. He told me to come in and shut the door. Since that amazing Stratton Oakmont Christmas party, we had both known that we shared a fierce animal attraction. I completely understood what lust was all about when I was near Glen.

I parked my ass on the corner of his desk. Glen seemed really distracted. When I looked at his face, I realized that he smelled pussy! What a dog.

It was now or never. I took his eager hand and guided it up my skirt. When he reached my wet lips, there was a sense of relief in both of us. We finally had our chance. Would he go for it? His finger was long, strong, and hard. He wanted more and I wanted it instantly. But there? Why not? The blinds were closed. He grabbed me, pulled me next to him, and kissed me, hard. It was one of those wet, sloppy, intense kisses.

"I want to eat you so badly, you sexy bitch."

"Baby, you know what I want. Give it to me hard."

There was no stopping him now. Before I knew what happened, Glen was inside me and it felt good, so good. I had imagined Glen as the type who could last all night, but he came fast. I couldn't believe it. Glen sensed my disappointment and continued with his hands. He knew exactly where to touch me, pumping in and out with that one hard finger. I was so turned on that I had to muffle my own screams. Glen reminded me that it was the middle of the day and that Josh could return at any minute. I looked at him one last time and heaved a sigh. What a shame that he was married to that pig. He was such a fine specimen.

I made up my mind that I would have Glen again, and soon. On the desk, under the desk, in the desk—it doesn't matter. You will be mine, if only for the night.

I left Glen's office thinking that he could at least have waited until I came. I was so close! Glen was probably afraid that I would be heard by the brokers, or that Josh would return. Not that either one of them probably really cared, but Stratton did have a policy that the office was a sex-free zone while the market was open. As I was leaving I thought about how drenched Glen was with sweat. At the same time I recalled the freshly starched shirts that were always hanging on the wall. This would certainly be classified as an *Aha!* moment. I was so frustrated. If he'd been the one left wanting, Glen could masturbate in his office and no one would know. But where could I go? I needed relief badly.

The ladies room! I thought of Glen and his oversized fingers and I wondered just how big his dick was. Six or seven inches was my guess, but it had been such a quickie that I had barely had a chance to think about it, and never had a chance to see. I had also failed to get any advice about going out on my own, but that didn't matter; I already knew that Glen would advise me to leave the Bott. He would never openly bash the Bott, but I was certain that there were issues between the Bott and Glen. Major issues.

I decided to keep working for the Bott just a little longer. The Bott and his partner, Steven Goldberg, were two of the largest producers at Stratton Oakmont. They had a great model for success and I wanted to make sure I mastered it before I was on my own. I had asked the Bott about their approach. I wasn't sure he would answer since he usually ducked my questions and told me to look things up myself, but it wasn't really a financial question but a marketing question. And like so many men, the Bott was happy to brag about his success; suddenly he had all the time in the world.

"Here's the strategy that has worked for me, Ginger. Cold callers make the first contact with the prospective client. They write up the lead. The account openers take the lead and try to turn it into an account. After one of my account openers actually opens a new account, I am their next contact. The customer is pleasantly surprised when I call and don't recommend stock. My role is to tee up Steven Goldberg, my partner," said the Bott. "When I get Mr. Jones on the phone, I talk a *big* game. First, I thank them for opening an account with Stratton Oakmont. Then I tell Mr. Jones that I would like to ask one of the principals of the firm, Mr. Goldberg, to review their account personally, and that he might possibly call them. I tell them that it is *doubtful* that he will call them because he is a very busy man who spends most of his day analyzing the Fibonacci numbers, evaluating the support levels, and determining where the resistance is," said the Bott. "And then I say, 'If I can convince him to call you, I beg you, please, please take his call. It will be worth your while.'"

How could anyone turn an offer like that down? Even someone who was left thinking that the Bott was full of shit would think, "Ah, but maybe that Goldberg guy might be worth listening to. He might have some good tips."

Steven Goldberg was a short Jewish kid from Great Neck with a golden voice. He was about twenty-five. He had one of the deepest, most powerful voices in the company, and he spoke with such confidence that his customers were certain that he must know what he was doing. And that was what mattered: the clients just had to believe the brokers.

When I heard that Steven was from Great Neck, I remembered the years that I lived there, and the first time Freddy had come to my apartment in Great Neck. He had walked in and kissed me hello. He was raring to go, as usual, and he was there no more than five minutes when he had broken the sphinx that I had carried home from a trip to Greece. I was furious! It was not that I cared about the stupid statue so much but that Freddy was so nonchalant about it. He didn't give a shit that he had broken it, and he never apologized. I should have guessed then, and would learn later in our marriage, that that was Freddy's usual method of dealing with that type of incident. And it apparently was not an isolated incident, but something that happened to him regularly. Freddy was a klutz from a family of klutzes. Every one of them would, without exception, eventually break something that was mine.

It took a while for him to get to the point where he found it funny, but Freddy finally learned to joke about his accident-prone family, saying things like, "We used to wear raincoats at dinner!" He was the proverbial bull in a china shop. Freddy never walked into a room; he stomped into it. God forbid I would want to sleep late if he was already up. It had always been a mystery to me how he could be so smooth on the dance floor, when any other time he was constantly tripping over my feet and stepping on my toes.

But in those early days, I didn't care. We went from club to club, dancing our life away. Then, just when it seemed that my feet could take no more abuse, along came my second child, Brian, and Freddy and I put our dancing on hold for a while, well we cut back anyway to occasional weekends. It was difficult to dance when we were up all night attending to a screaming newborn!

It was a rare occasion for Freddy and I to go out dancing after Brian was born. Then one night, we decided to get a babysitter and go out to celebrate our third anniversary. We were out dancing at a place in Port Washington, and had been on the dance floor for *maybe* fifteen minutes when a little hottie approached me. I was caught completely off guard.

She was probably seventeen years old with not an ounce of fat on her. She certainly had never carried two children. She was tall with perfectly straight, jet-black hair, with the look of a typical Latino. I guessed, considering the town we were in and the jewelry she wore, that she was Jewish. And of course the deck was stacked: she had a pair of the finest breasts money could buy. They couldn't possibly have been real.

She approached me without fear or hesitation. "I am very young," she said to me.

I almost said, "Do I fuckin' care?"

But before I could say anything, she said, "I recently took dance lessons. Do you mind if I dance with him?"

I was about to ask, "Are you fucking crazy?" when I was stunned into silence.

Freddy replied for me. "Okay!"

I was so mad that the bitch ruined our night. I could not get over it. And it seemed like after that night, we couldn't go *anywhere* without some other woman asking Freddy for a dance. It didn't matter if it was a club, a wedding, or a party—there was always some bitch waiting for her chance to cut in. I felt so uncomfortable around such women. They were all so arrogant; it was unbelievable. They seemed to feel that because he was a great dancer, Fred was public property! Apparently I was supposed to feel sorry for them because they had taken lessons and knew the steps, but their husbands or boyfriends hated to dance, so they didn't have a dance partner. Did they not get it? If *they* danced with Freddy, that meant that *I* did not have a dance partner. It seemed to be getting worse lately.

The last time we'd gone out, I was approached by the singer of the band we were dancing to, and asked, "Do you share?"

I thought I would explode! *You must be kidding! Go away!* But all I said was, "No. Absolutely not." The prettier they were, the more aggressive they were, especially if they could dance.

Soon I found myself with all kinds suspicions running through my head. I thought, "Maybe I needed to work closer to home in a more stable environment." And that was one reason why I stayed at Stratton Oakmont. I knew that something was going on. If I worked closer to home, I could catch him.

———— ✖ ————

New accounts! New accounts! New accounts!

My personal goal was a hat-trick—three new accounts—every day. It was nearly impossible to open three accounts every day, so some days I didn't make my goal. But I got a hat trick often enough that many of the other brokers were starting to respect me, and of course some were starting to hate me. If someone could pop a hat trick, Frankie made a big deal over it. I eventually realized that customers "lost" money so rapidly that we always needed a fresh supply of new accounts. *Churn and burn.* As hard as I tried to do the right thing, it seemed almost impossible to do.

When the climate at Stratton Oakmont began its downward spiral, Frankie went down with it. Or maybe Frankie's downward spiral initiated the demise of the company. Either way, he was certainly on a downhill roll. His Quaalude habit had raged out of control. His meetings had become complete circuses. His outrageous behavior included midget throwing, head shaving, trumpet playing, and lots of crazy, crazy stuff. Everything that people heard about Stratton Oakmont was true and then some.

I had just had another hat-trick day. Frankie had launched the afternoon meeting, and his theme of the day was what to say to customers when stocks were down. The reason for his topic was, unfortunately, that all our stocks were down. Every one of them. My customers hated me. What a way to start a new business.

"You can't be concerned about day-to-day blips in the stock market. Stocks trade. Do not overanalyze it. You run the risk of paralysis by analysis. People make money in good and bad markets. The bulls and the bears eat. The pigs get slaughtered."

I guess he never listened to his own advice. The pigs get *slaughtered.* Frankie was so stoned and out of control on that particular day that his capo had to grab the mike and get him the hell out of there. "I don't get it. Customers call me up and say, 'I lost my money!' I lost my money? What are they talking about? I know *exactly* where their money is! It's in my bank account!"

That was the moment that he was dragged out of the boardroom and probably given an ice-cold shower and a gallon of coffee. Frankie had admitted to the room that he was nothing more than a thief. I was determined to get out of there ASAP. I was not going to go to jail!

Stay the course. Failure is not an option.

I had once watched a young man work out in my gym. His entire workout consisted of one exercise: he would pile several steps one on top of the other. He jumped up, landing with both feet on top of the step, then jumped down. I was fascinated by this exercise and asked him what happened if he missed the step, which would have been a disaster. He looked at me and said in an official military voice, "Failure is not an option."

That became my mantra. *Failure is not an option.* Bad day at work? *Failure is not an option.* Focusing on those words for some reason helped me through the day. It was tough out there.

I was in the boardroom one Saturday cold calling. The man who answered the phone was really friendly, even when I said I was from Stratton Oakmont. I was always surprised when the prospects were friendly. When I asked, "How is your broker doing for you?" I was shocked to hear his response: "Not nearly as good as Stratton Oakmont is." Obviously, the man already *had* had an account with us. Still following my script, I asked him for the name of his broker, and he said, "Glen Polansky." I told him that he was in good hands, and was about to hang up when he said, "Can I ask you a question? How long have you been working there?"

I answered that it was going on two years.

"I find it so strange that every time Glen tells me to sell something, the minute I do, the stock goes straight down," the man said.

"Glen is a top producer for Stratton. He really watches his accounts and his customer's positions," I said cautiously. "Glen is also really good at what he does." I wanted to add, "Do me a favor and call me the next time Glen tells you to sell something!"

I found the call disturbing. Even the customers had noticed that something funny was going on. I went to my friend Sal to get his thoughts.

"Even the customers notice," I said. "That's bad."

Sal started talking about stock manipulation. He explained that the brokers at Stratton Oakmont were there to provide liquidity for the principals of the firm, not to make money for the customers. "Don't you get it? *You* are the firm's liquidity. If there was bad news on a company that we were involved with, Frankie needed to get the big boys out of their stock,. He could not risk having his personal clients lose money and these stocks were typically illiquid. If his client dumped a big position, it could cause a chain reaction. That would not only cause the stock to tank but could adversely affect all the Stratton Oakmont stocks. Frankie would paythe brokers an extra rip in the stock.. as an incentive. So in addition to the spread, he might offer, for example, a buck in the stock. It was easy to do gross when there was a buck in it. If your customer bought fifty thousand shares, you would do $50,000 gross and net $25,000! Not a bad deal. Of course, the customers were buying worthless stock and would most likely lose all their money.

"When the brokers are buying, the principals are selling," said Sal. "And to take it a step further, you're buying their customer's stock so that they are *able* to sell."

I felt so stupid and used. I was angry. That was bullshit! I swore that I would never buy another Stratton Oakmont stock again.

Of course, that was what I told myself on that particular day, but it was not exactly what I did. Frankie had a way of motivating us, getting us to believe, when all hope was gone. Whether he was telling the truth or lying, he had this way of whipping the room into a frenzy. I wanted so badly to believe.

"We're the best brokers on the street. We do the best deals! We're *bad*! We're Stratton fuckin' Oakmont!"

7

THE LARGEST CASINO IN THE WORLD

ALTHOUGH I HAD talked about it many times, it was not until the summer of 1995 that I actually went out on my own. I finally felt confident enough to make the move away from the Bott and go my separate way. I had enough leads squirreled away to get started. I had spent many long hours cold calling every day so that I would have a huge backlog of leads. And so, I began the tedious battle of building up a business. Now that I was on my own, it was my responsibility to get leads as well as open accounts. I was the boss. I made all the decisions. At least, that was what I wanted to believe.

One month later, I was feeling lost and scared.

I seemed to have a book full of pikers and absolutely no whales. Whales were the big money. Pikers were the small investors, the ones with less than a hundred grand in the market, who drove us nuts. It didn't matter if they sent us a hundred dollars or a thousand dollars, they would call us constantly. Frankie had a solution for that. Every time they called, we were supposed to try to sell them something else! It worked like a charm. Eventually they stopped calling.

No one wanted to deal with piker midgets: they were annoying, bothersome assholes. *Piker midget assholes.* The problem was, I could never be sure that a piker midget asshole wasn't a whale in hiding or the millionaire next door. Given that there were reputed to be a million millionaires in the United States in the '90s, I was bound to get *some* whales. Most clients lied about how much money they were investing, so you never knew, for sure. I heard the story of one broker who had opened a new account with a guy who whined throughout the entire process that he had no money. He was second-traded into a house stock, and he told the broker that he wasn't sure if he had the funds to cover the four grand that was due for his thousand-share trade. Then the stock popped up a quarter, and the customer decided he needed to add to his position…and sent the broker a million dollars. One million dollars! Nothing was ever really certain.

In the short period of time that I had been on my own, I had focused on opening as many new accounts as I could. I was popping new accounts like crazy. I was on a mission. After a dozen or so accounts, I got Dr. Ebert on the phone and gave him the Dr Pepper pitch. That was the beginning of our long and sometimes rocky relationship.

After three months of being on my own, I was sitting by myself in the boardroom when I was approached by another female broker. "So, Ginger, how's it going?"

"It's going well, thanks. It's a little scary doing it on my own," I said.

Her name was Roni Van Brunt. She was the same age as I, but taller, with bleached-blond hair that she wore really straight with bangs, sort of an aging all-American California look. When she wore her hair in a ponytail, she reminded me of a younger Anna Keller, the Nazi office manager. Although she was not fat, she probably had thirty pounds on me. Roni was divorced and pretty lonely, I could tell. A real princess.

"Yeah, it's pretty scary at first," she said. "I've been here four years, so I'm used to it now. How long were you with the Bott?"

"Including the time I spent as his cold caller, almost a year," I said. "He was really great to work for. I kind of regret that I left him."

"I noticed that you've been kicking ass lately. How many new accounts have you opened?"

"Probably twenty-five or thirty."

"Wow. That is incredible! The reason that I wanted to talk to you is that I was wondering if you would be interested in forming a partnership, kind of a Bott-Goldberg deal. I'm really great at second trading, but I suck at opening new accounts," she said. "If you're interested, we could combine our books and have a phenomenal business. The Bott and Goldberg will need to step aside as top dogs! Oh, and if we need help, my brother is head trader here. He's been unbelievably supportive. It has definitely helped to have him on my side!"

"It sounds great! My knee-jerk reaction is to say yes. How about I sleep on it and tell you tomorrow?"

"Fabulous!" As Roni walked away, I noticed that she wore very tight black pants and a Chanel-type check jacket, probably from Saks or Bloomies, that was to die for. If her taste in clothes was any sign of how well we might work together, I took that as a good omen.

Roni stopped by my desk the next day. I was pumped. I suggested that we sign a formal partnership agreement, which Roni thought that was a great idea. To do it officially, we needed Frankie to approve it. Since I was skilled at opening accounts and Roni said that her expertise was in second trading, we didn't think he would have a problem. Roni had hit me at my weakest moment, when I was sure that my new business consisted of all piker midgets. I wanted the security of having another person to strategize with and—I'm not gonna lie—also for the coke. Roni *always* had the best cocaine. Mind-blowing stuff!

Frankie thought it was a great idea. Well, that was what Roni told me when she came out of his office. "Ginger, let's celebrate! We have a deal. We are going to be unstoppable!" she said. "Come on, everyone's going to Millie's Place for lunch."

Millie's was a Great Neck institution that featured The Big Salad. We are talking *huge*. But the funniest thing was, since it was 99 percent iceberg lettuce, I always left there hungry.

"Hey, Ginger, come with me to the ladies room." We walked into their bathroom and Roni motioned to follow her into a stall. She whipped out a hundred-dollar bill, a small mirror, and some of the best cocaine that I had ever seen. She pulled a razor blade from her purse to refine it so that we wouldn't destroy our noses and so she could cut it into lines.

By the time we left Millie's and got back to the office, we were SO wasted. I moved my seat next to Roni's and the Rogers-Van Brunt team was born. What a mistake. It was a premature birth: neither of us was in any shape to call customers.

Frankie had moved the previous occupant of my new desk to the front of the room. Everyone was warned about sitting the front. It was definitely in the combat zone! Frankie usually threw his infamous temper tantrums up in the front of the room. Anyone whose seat was there needed thick skin and good ducking skills!

It was an incredibly fun day. That had been the first time that I had gone *out* to lunch in a really long time. I quickly learned, though, that what I considered an unusual day was not at all unusual for Roni. She spent almost every day exactly the same way.

"How do you want to proceed? What's our game plan?" I asked.

"Let me think about it," she said. "How about tomorrow we take a look at your book?"

It didn't take me long to figure out that Roni had no business. Her customers were toasted: down in every stock they owned and not thrilled with Roni. She came across as a complete bitch on the phone, which did not exactly endear her to either her customers or mine. And because Roni was incredibly lazy, she had not opened a new account in months. New accounts were essential to building a business at Stratton Oakmont.

I spent the first day of our new partnership calling all my clients and teeing up Roni in a big way. It was the Bott-Goldberg strategy, which had worked so well for them. Everyone wanted to copy it. It made sense at the time. I'd had a wonderful teacher for the last year, and now it was my chance to shine. I was very surprised, but in a strange way I was thrilled by my clients' response.

Dr. Ebert was a great example. "Good morning, Dr. Ebert. Ginger Rogers, Stratton Oakmont. How are you today?"

"I'm okay. What's happening with my Dr Pepper?" I knew the clients had money when they had no idea where their stocks were trading.

"Things look great! You're up three points in the position," I said. "The reason I'm calling today is to tell you that I have a new business partner. Her name is Roni Van Brunt. She's one of the top female traders on the street.". Fortunately he never asked me what street!

"Well, congratulations."

"Roni spends most of her day analyzing the fundamentals of stocks. She evaluates the support and resistance of a stock. She even looks at the moving average and Fibonacci numbers. She'll probably give you a call, just to introduce herself when she has some time."

"Well, okay. But I really want to deal with you!"

What could I say? I was adorable.

Although our plan was that I would focus on opening accounts, Roni would also attempt to open accounts—if she was not hung over from the night before, high, or just too lazy. She and I were opening accounts with the Dr Pepper pitch, my all-time favorite sales pitch, and during my partnership with Roni, that particular take-over that we were predicting actually happened! We looked like freakin' geniuses. It was great. Typically, when the first stock went up, it was easy to second-trade clients...except that when Roni the bitch was unleashed on them, they were unprepared for her and usually unreceptive. There was, however, one Asian dude who responded to Roni; she convinced him to take ten thousand shares of a company called SMTV. I didn't happen to think that it was a great buy at eight dollars a share, but she insisted. Of course, there just happened to be a buck in the stock. We were on our way to riches and fame. When the stock ticked up, Chen bought another twenty thousand shares.

I was a great account opener, and Roni had told me that she was a great second trader. She was not, in fact, a great second trader. She was, in fact, a lazy bitch, which I began to suspect very early into our partnership. I also suspected that any success she'd had to date was, like everything else, just a numbers game. If we asked enough people to buy ten thousand shares of stock, eventually someone would say yes. Even a blind squirrel finds an acorn sometimes.

Life would have been wonderful...except that SMTV began to free fall. We were in trouble.

Glen came out of his office on a regular basis and addressed the troops. "I don't want *any* sell tickets on SMTV! *Hold them in.* This is why you get paid the big bucks! When a customer wants to sell, ask them to buy more! Mr. Customer, you liked the company at eight, you gotta love it at two. Let me say it again: No sell tickets!"

Roni was just a passable second trader, but ours started out as a fairly decent partnership, even though it wasn't due to any special skills that Roni brought to the table. The typical account that I opened was a nice sweet guy who liked me and wanted to trade with me! There were always some exceptions to the rule, though, like Mr. Chen, who had bought SMTV from Roni. Most customers will honor their verbal commitment and pay for the stock that they bought. However, every now and then, we would get customers who reneged on their trades and wouldn't pay. Roni second-traded one of my accounts into

SMTV, and the guy reneged on us. The settlement date for trades at that point was still seven days. A lot of shit can happen in seven days.

When he saw SMTV go down several points before the settlement date, Mr. Jones called our sales assistant, sold his Dr Pepper shares, and had a check for that sale cut and mailed immediately. Then he reneged on the SMTV trade. *Shit!* I knew that guy was a dirt bag! By the time we sold out of the position, we were down thirty grand. How would we ever recover? I leaned that most brokers walked when that happened to them. Fortunately for us, Roni had done some gross with Mr. Chen, one of my customers. That offset some of the loss. Unfortunately, for Mr. Chen, the gross that she did was in SMTV and Chen was down $150,000 and now wanted to sell.

What were we going to do? Roni went into Frankie's office and shut the door. I do not know what was said or done in there. But when she came out, we were off the hook and had the okay to sell! In addition, Frankie had agreed to cover a third of the hit, which gave us a hit of only ten thousand dollars each. *Only* ten thousand dollars. All our clients owned SMTV. So, in addition to us having to take the huge hit that month, all our clients were so mad about SMTV that Roni could not sell anything else to anyone.

Mr. Chen was madder than all hell. "I have never lost so much money in such a short period of time!" He never traded with Roni again.

We tried to get back to business as usual. *New accounts, new accounts, new accounts!* I was starting to understand why they were needed on a regular basis. I am not sure what it was but, for some reason, I became skilled at opening accounts with doctors. I was not sure why they liked me, but it seemed that they loved my voice. Doctors are notoriously bad investors, perhaps because so many of them think that they are smarter than everyone else. They were wary, though, because the fact that they were known to have big bucks made them a target for every con artist who could get them on the phone. When a doctor took my call, I was pretty certain I was *in*. Doctors were easily romanced by my sweet, sexy voice, and when I went for the kill, I could catch them completely off guard.

All the brokers at Stratton Oakmont searched for their whales—the one guy who would send in the money. My whale was a doctor. I found my whale during my partnership with Roni Van Brunt. It was Dr. Ebert. Neither Roni nor I *knew* that he was a whale. We knew that he had two million dollars invested with Merrill Lynch, but he was *not* sending that kind of money to Stratton Oakmont. When our partnership broke up, Roni would have kept him if she thought that he would trade with her. Unfortunately for her—and fortunately for me—Dr. Ebert did not respond to Roni's voice or her style. He would not second-trade because he did not like Roni. In fact, Roni had a difficult time second-trading many of the accounts that I opened: my customers thought that they would be dealing with sweet Ginger Rogers, and did not like being completely blindsided by the whining bitch who was unleashed on them.

I believed that the reason that Frankie covered half the SMTV hit was that Roni had been at the firm four years—an eternity at Stratton Oakmont—and because her brother was head trader. At the end of the month, after working my ass off for an entire month, the Rogers-Van Brunt team did zero gross. In other words, we did not earn any commission. How would we stand up in front of everyone in the boardroom and announce a big fat goose egg? Simple. Roni would lie!

My paycheck was zero for the month. I was stunned and furious. Roni could see that, and she vowed to do whatever she had to do to make money the next month. And that she did. To make up for the miserable month, she bought, sold, and flipped-flopped everything and anything like freakin' flapjacks. If there was a buck in a stock, she bought it. It didn't matter what the company did or which clients she recommended the stock to; she was a woman on a mission. And that mission was to hold onto the account-opening goose who was laying the golden eggs she was frying. I was really disgusted with her. I knew that first month that I should break off our partnership, but I was scared it might get ugly. And there was still that one special thing that Roni did bring to the partnership: she still always had the *best* cocaine. And she had been able to get Frankie to cover half of the hit. So, I kept working with Roni—longer than I should have. But the end of our relationship was near. I knew it, and I knew that Roni knew it.

8

How Is Your U4?

I ALWAYS FOUND it absurd that the NASD was self-regulated. The NASD was the parent company of NASD Regulation, Inc., and the NASDAQ stock exchange. Their responsibility was to ensure that the rules were followed, which they tried to accomplish by policing the market. Their responsibilities included registration, education, testing, and examination of member firms and their employees. The NASD also had oversight of market-making activities and trading practices, regulating the trading activity of their members.

Stratton Oakmont loved to dance the fine line between uncommon sales practices and outright illegal sales practices. They practiced an in-your-face methodology that pushed the NASD to their limits of tolerance. It's probable that Stratton Oakmont's demise and the implosion of the NASD that led to their being restructured as FINRA, as well as the introduction of a host of new and more restrictive laws, were inexorably linked to one another. In the past, the NASD had probably operated largely on the assumption that brokers were working on behalf of their clients. I doubt that they had ever suspected the possibility of a brokerage firm that used clients to work on behalf of their own profit center. Of course, there were always one or two rogue brokers at any firm, but at Stratton Oakmont the number of rogues was closer to four or five hundred—basically the entire firm. When the NASD found themselves becoming overwhelmed by the number of complaints that they were receiving daily about Stratton Oakmont, they apparently decided to make an example of them that would serve as a warning to other firms and their brokers.

My problems with the NASD was that they allowed commissioned brokers in the stock market and that they did not operate by the same rules as a normal court. I had read an article on insider trading that said, basically, if you thought something was illegal, then it most likely *was* illegal, even if there was no law pertaining to that specific situation. *Huh?*

When it came to illegalities, and new methods of scamming people, Stratton Oakmont most likely inspired an entire chapter in the law books!

The laws required that brokers separate their need for income from the clients' needs. Their suitability, goals, and objectives should be the brokers' only consideration. *Bullshit!* I had a need to pay my mortgage, a need to fund my sons' education, and a need to eat! How could I possibly put those concerns aside and care more about losing some dude's money? If I worried about losing money, I ran the risk of analysis paralysis. Frankie said that all the time. Great brokers make money in a good or a bad market. The bulls *and* the bears eat.

I vowed that I would not let the downturn in the market get to me. Paralysis by analysis would not get me. I wanted to make the customers money, but it became clear to me that in the roach motel, client profits were the exception, not the rule. When our clients called in a panic because of the price of a stock and wanted to sell, we were told by Frankie to hold them in.

"That's why you get paid the big bucks. Hold them in!"

At Stratton Oakmont, it was all about the money. At the end of every month, when Frankie went around the room with his mike, not one single broker stood up and announced that he or she had done zero gross for the month. If any of them had the nerve to say zero, they would not want to get up more than once and make that announcement, believe me.. When we didn't pull in the big commission, we had the feeling that we were letting the firm, letting the family down. It was devastating. We were so brainwashed with the mafia-family bullshit that we felt worse for letting down the Stratton Oakmont family than we felt going home to our real families and telling them we had zeroed out. *We're bad! We're Stratton fuckin' Oakmont!*

I finally experienced first-hand how the prices were held at a certain level. Although I was never denied a sell, I did *not* want to go in with a block of stock unless I knew in advance that it would be okay. The irony was that if we were allowed to sell a block at Stratton Oakmont, that meant that the principals were looking for that stock, and the chances were good that it would go up the minute we unloaded it. *Hold them in! That's why you make the big bucks!* I felt completely helpless and disgusted. I knew the writing was on the wall, and that I would have to get out of there.

When we finally got a paycheck the month after we zeroed out, in an effort to make the situation a little more bearable, Roni turned to me. "Come on, Ginger. Let's get high! I scored some coke that you have to try."

I was never one to pass on an opportunity like that. "Sure, let's check it out," I said, though I really was not very enthusiastic. She took me into the ladies room and whipped out her stash. What a fuckin' stash she had! Cocaine was one of the oldest known drugs in existence, and it was still the drug of choice in the '90s. It was really popular with people like brokers because it was a powerful stimulant and we were in an elite group: we could afford it.

Roni opened her purse and took out her mirror, razor blade, a crisp hundred-dollar bill, and several grams of cocaine. It was a beautiful, fine, white, crystalline powder that looked just like snow. It was up our noses in seconds.

Suddenly I felt so much better about everything. Maybe I should give Roni another chance?

I was not sure how long Stratton Oakmont would be around. Why should it be any different? Almost every firm that I had ever worked for no longer existed. After my tumultuous month, I did what I had always done when I sensed that the company where I worked might be in trouble: I started to explore my options. Our paychecks, despite all the churning that Roni had done, was a measly two thousand dollars each—barely better than what the Bott had paid me. So when I saw an ad for a position at Prudential, I decided to go for an interview.

The position was for a junior broker, which I new was a glorified name for a licensed cold caller. I didn't care. I wanted out of the family. Taking a job on Wall Street would mean a return to commuting into Manhattan, but I would do whatever it took.

When I arrived at the Prudential office, I laughed out loud. Now that was how I pictured the reception area of a financial institution: hand-woven Persian carpets, mahogany paneling, a luxurious mahogany desk, Oriental vases—they had it all. I was meeting with Joel Green, the head broker to whom I would be reporting. Joel came out in a white shirt with dark trousers and a very conservative tie. The only hip thing about Joel was his sandy hair, which he wore slicked back a la Gordon Gecko. It was part of the uniform that all male brokers wore to show that they carried a big stick!

Joel asked me many questions about the market, which I easily answered. I had learned a great deal working at Stratton Oakmont. Joel asked me to wait in the conference room. He wanted to introduce me to his partner, Ron Gardner.

I immediately hit it off with Ron. He was a 6'2 hunk of a man. I could tell that both brokers loved me! They had never met anyone like me, and they wanted to know how soon I could start. I was thrilled! It was exactly the type of break that I needed. Then they asked me a question that I could not answer.

"How's your U4?" Joel asked.

"Fine, thank you!" I said. "How's yours?" They started laughing.

I did not have a *clue* what they were talking about! They told me that I would know if there was a problem, because the firm was required to inform a broker if a customer complained, but that they would look into it for me. The guy from Prudential called me the next day to tell me that they had not found a problem…they had found *four* problems. There were *four* complaints against me. How could that be possible? I had pretty decent relationships with my customers. Were they down in their positions? Yes, for the most part they *were* down and losing money, but there was nothing I could do about that. When I was finally able to see the complaints, they were all exactly what I feared and suspected: they were not about me, but about Roni. There was not a single complaint that even mentioned my name except as the person who opened the account. I knew that my customers did not like Roni or her bullying style. When I asked compliance at Stratton Oakmont what was going on, I was told that since Roni and I were officially partners, we had a joint U4. That meant that any complaint that came in would be on both of our records. I was furious!

That was the last straw…. I decided I had to end our partnership immediately before any more damage could be done. When I returned to Stratton Oakmont, I saw Roni fooling around at her desk. I remembered the advice that my sister gave me for situations like this Keep your cool. He who loses his temper, loses the argument. It was true. More importantly, the longer you keep your cool, the madder your opponent will be. Roni must have seen that there was steam coming out of my head, because she immediately hung up the phone.

"Ginger, what's wrong?"

"We need to talk. Can we meet in the 'conference room' in fifteen minutes? I need to talk to Glen first."

"Sure. Okay."

I knocked on Glen's door and did not wait for him to bark his usual "Enter please". I was so angry that I just did not care. I walked in. I was relieved that he was alone.

"Ginger, baby, what's wrong?" Glen could read me like a book.

"I thought it was a good idea. I thought it would work. But man, she is a *worthless* piece of *shit*."

"Oh, boy. I'll tell Frankie. Okay, I have a new desk for you. It's right by Tommy. You'll learn a lot from him."

"In the front of the room?"

"You'll be fine."

"Who is going to split our book?"

"Frankie always does that so he can take any whales for himself."

I considered calling Dr. Ebert to give him a heads-up, but Roni was waiting for me. I walked into the ladies room—AKA the 'conference room'—and joined Roni on the floor. I was so angry that I knew that if I remained standing, I would explode. The bathroom was clean but still just a basic public restroom. Although it belonged to the building, it was on our floor, and had not been renovated along with the restrooms on other floors. This room was typical Stratton Oakmont. Why waste money?

Roni had coked up for the occasion.

"Hi, Ginger. What's goin' on, lady?"

"Were you aware that we have complaints against us?"

She nodded.

"Really? And you were going to share that information with me...when?"

"Ginger, I knew you would be mad. The complaints are such total bullshit! Especially that Bernie asshole. What a dick. Anyway, we have them all on tape. Frankie will get our lawyers after them. It's cool."

"It is *not* cool. Guys here are getting dragged into arbitration left and right and are paying big fines. I don't know about you, but I don't have an extra twenty thousand dollars sitting around that I would like to donate to the SEC!"

"Frankie is *not* going to let us pay a fee like that!"

"I can't count on that. Going to trial is not something that I care to do."

"Frankie will defend us, you'll see. It will be fine."

"Well, I don't think so. What if my friends find out? Or my family? Or my customers? This could ruin my career!"

"Ginger, don't be such a fuckin' drama queen. I told you, Frankie will take care of this. He has plenty of money set aside for these nuisance suits."

"Well, anyway, Roni, I really don't think that our partnership is working out."

"Huh? What?"

"It's no good. I'm working twice as hard as I was before and not making *any* money. And now this? It will be better for both of us if we call it a day. I'm going back out on my own."

I heard Roni say under her breath, "You fuckin' bitch."

I told myself that it was essential to stay calm, and keep cool. I said nothing.

"Well if that's how you feel, that is just *fuckin' fine* with me!" Roni shrieked. She got up from the floor and slammed her fist into one of the stall doors for emphasis. "I don't need you! I *never* needed you! You open nothing but *midget assholes* that won't trade, like that worthless piece of shit Bernie. Well, he may have complained but at least he second-traded."

I couldn't help myself. "Yeah. He second-traded because I second-traded him!"

"Fuck you!" Roni said. "You can keep your fuckin' crybaby Brad and that worthless prick, Dr. Ebert. Your customers are a bunch of losers. In fact, I'm *glad* that we lost them so much money. The only exception is Mr. Chen, and don't even *think about* asking for his account. All your customers *suck dick*! They have been nothing but fuckin' nightmares. I *never* had complaints before I met you. Oh, and by the way, don't think for a minute that you're going to decide who you keep. I'll ask Frankie to divide our book. You can keep all your midget customers that you had before—they're worthless anyway, just a bunch of renegers. I'll keep mine, and we'll split the ones we opened since we have been together!"

I thought about asking her which accounts *we* had opened, but figured I better not. Roni was about to explode. She grabbed her Chanel bag. As she was leaving, she said, "After all the fuckin' coke I turned you on to? This is the thanks I get? Oh, yeah, and I want all of my leads back." I thought that I saw a tiny little tear make its way down over that Chanel-encrusted foundation of hers. But she turned too quickly for me to confirm it.

And just like that, it was over. I ended our joint venture and was going on my own once again. And so we split the business in two. As we discussed in the ladies room, we would both keep the customers that we had before the partnership. I let Roni keep Mr. Chen—she thought that she could sell him anything, but I sensed that he was done—and I was able to keep Dr. Ebert, since Roni was convinced that he was a piker midget asshole because she couldn't second-trade him. The breakup had been about as ugly as I had imagined it would be. Roni left the ladies room crying and muttering, "That bitch! That fuckin' bitch! After all I did for her, this is how she treats me. She'll get hers."

Fortunately, Frankie agreed with Glen about where I was going to move. He was happy to immediately relocate me.

I grabbed my stuff and moved as fast as I possibly could out from under Roni's watchful eye. In true Stratton Oakmont style, Frankie said, "Take Pat Mulligan's desk. He's no longer here."

Evidently, that was not exactly true. Pat walked in five minutes later. "Ginger? Is there a reason that you're sitting at my desk?" Then it dawned on him. He was getting fired.

I didn't know what to say. "Well, uh. Frankie told me to sit here, and to send you in to see him. So you need to talk to Frankie." I did not have a good poker face. He knew that his ass was grass. I never saw Pat Mulligan again.

I'd been worried about sitting up front, but I liked sitting next to Tommy, learning how he did gross. Tommy, like many of the other largest producers at Stratton Oakmont, did his gross by flip-flopping and bebopping his customers. In other words, they churned their accounts. In the brokerage world, churning is the word for excessive trading. It is illegal. The large brokers did their gross by selling blocks for eighths and quarters. Think about that. If a broker was long fifty thousand shares of any dog-shit stock and took an eighth and moved on, that was six grand in profit! Do that five times and that would be thirty grand a month. *Yeah, baby.* The clients didn't care. If we were making them money, the clients looked the other way. Why do you think it took years to catch my friend Bernie Madoff down in Boca? When we gave the clients the upper hand, everyone was happy.

Nobody likes to lose. That is why the '90s were so incredible. The *Wall Street Journal* would match its stock picks, obtained by a dart-throwing monkey, to a professional analyst's picks to see which one outperformed the other and the market, expecting the pro to prevail. In the '90s, though, just about anything that investors bought went up. It went up in a big way.

There is a theory known as the average investor theory, which holds that that it's time to sell when average investors start offering stock advice. When taxi drivers, mail carriers, and coffee vendors start giving out stock tips, it's time to sell every stock and sit in cash. The average investor theory flashed in my head one night that summer, almost like a warning. I was having dinner in Manhattan with some friends who were celebrating the huge increases that a particular technology stock in their portfolio had seen over the past year. The meteoric rise of the stock had made everyone at the table so much money that they joked about taking a helicopter home. *Beware the average investor.*

9

NICE TRADE

THE MEETINGS HAD been getting bad before, but lately they had seemed completely out of control, probably as a result of combining five hundred brokers with a seemingly limitless supply of 'ludes and cocaine. Frankie was so strung out that his message had been the same at three meetings in a row: "We're a family. You are so lucky to be here! It is an honor and a privilege to work here. You will never make money anywhere else. We do the best deals! Stratton fuckin' Oakmont!" The same message that used to leave me feeling excited and energized though was beginning to leave me feeling angry and manipulated.

Then when I got home, I had to turn off that anger so it didn't burn my family. Poor darling Freddy; he really was such a patient man. I would walk into my house every night at ten or so and say either, "Where's my fuckin' dinner?" or "Where the fuck is my dinner?"

I made Freddy cook for the entire family, even though he had recently had rotator-cuff surgery. "I'm sorry, dear. I don't have much sympathy for tennis injuries just now." After all, did Freddy care that I worked at Animal House? Well, let me say that he had no problem cashing the monthly commission check.

In the mid-1990s, every stock investors bought went up. Yet at Stratton Oakmont, the stocks that we were recommending were crashing all around us. My book was so blown up that there was only one thing that I could possibly do: *Open new accounts, new accounts, new accounts.*

I needed them, for sure. I had finally been able to see a copy of the complaints that were lodged against Roni and me. I was certain that my customers understood the risks involved in buying stock. When they were down, they could handle it better if their broker at least *pretended* to be somewhat sympathetic. Roni had no sympathy for anyone and couldn't even fake it, and that came across over the phone.

The first complaint was from Charles Wilson in Georgia. How I had managed to open an account with that Southern gentleman, I had no idea, but I did know that his beef was with Roni. He hated the bitch and felt that she had high-pressured him. We both sent him letters of apology assuring him that it would never happen again, and that was the end of that. Then there was Sid Cohen, a New York attorney who complained that an unauthorized trade had been done in his account. And, by the way, he happened to be down in the position. According to Cohen, the position that he was up in had been authorized, but the position that he was down in had not. I decided to confront him. When he got on the phone, I asked him if he recalled that all our conversations had been recorded. There was dead silence, and then he asked what I wanted him to do. "Rescind the complaint." He did it immediately, end of discussion.

At that point, Stratton Oakmont was being threatened by dozens of lawsuits. Frankie was both defiant and fearless. He would scream "buyers are liars!" as if that justified stealing. When clients really got pissed off, his response was typically belligerent. "They want to sue me? Bring it on! I got a floor full of Jewish lawyers that would love to get a hold of them. Bring it on!"

It was starting to get a little creepy there. Frankie had two full-time, armed security guards; he had apparently been getting death threats. I had heard that Jared Bellmore kept armed bodyguards on patrol on his block in Old Brookville. When the security guard at the front entrance to our boardroom quit, he was immediately replaced. His replacement just happened to be a midget security guard. Someone had a very sick sense of humor. I knew then for sure then that I was working in a fuckin' circus. The really funny part about it was that Frankie could not use his favorite line: *piker midget asshole!*

When he gave the meeting that day, he was in rare form. Actually, it was no longer rare for him, that totally wasted form. Stratton Oakmont must have been in more serious trouble than usual because Frankie decided that day to lock everyone in the boardroom until they raised some new money. But how could anyone do that? I was certain that everyone had the same positions as my customers. They were so crushed! But Frankie was out of control, completely mad, perhaps driven over the edge by the midget at the door. He wrote a number on the board: $500,000. Five hundred thousand dollars. Half a million dollars. Now I *knew* he was insane. Even today, that would be considered a large amount of money to raise, but in 1995 it was huge. Frankie was ranting and raving. He wanted new money. He needed new money. No one was permitted to leave the room until we got there.

"If you guys can't raise half a million dollars, then you're all a bunch of piker mmm-hmmm ah-hmmm!" Frankie started laughing so hard that he had to go into his office. The poor midget never knew that he was the brunt of the joke. Well, maybe he did.

Anyway, what could I do? My customers were all down. I went to all the usual suspects. No, no, no! No fuckin' way! I was pitching a company called MVSI, a company that I really felt would explode and had huge upside potential. What was I thinking?

What an idiot I had been. "Let's see. I haven't called Dr. Ebert in a while. He's never bought *anything* other than Dr Pepper. Oh, well, let's give it a shot."

I was lucky enough to get Dr. Ebert on the phone right away. I went at him *hard*. Tommy Renniger heard me battling a customer and jumped to my aid. From that point on, I have no recollection of what I said to Dr Ebert. Tommy fed me every line. Compliant or not, I simply repeated everything that Tommy said. One by one, we put away every objection. All Tommy had to do was get me started on a rebuttal, and I would take it from there. I focused so hard on Tommy's face, I almost went into uncontrollable giggles. I had to: if I took my eyes off his face, I'd be watching him grab his balls! When Tommy got nervous, he grabbed his balls.

After ten minutes or so of trying to convince Dr. Ebert to buy fifty thousand shares of MVSI stock, it was time to bring out my new secret weapon. When he mentioned that he did not want to lose money, I told him not to worry. "I will guide you IN to the market and guide you OUT of the market. Guide you IN, guide you OUT...and make you money!"

Ooh, baby, that was hot! I don't know if it's possible to hear drool, but I think I heard it. I stuck with my original pitch of fifty thousand shares, and never wavered. I knew he had the money. When he told me that he wanted to think about it, I knew he was mine.

"Dr. Ebert, pricing and timing are the tools of my trade. Take them away from me and you have an order taker at Charles Schwab. I can assure you that I am no order taker! You are tying my hands behind my back! I'll place a virtual stop-loss on the position and watch this stock like a hawk. If it ticks down even a quarter point, I'm on the phone with you. Go with fifty thousand shares. I will not let you down."

A long silence followed. *He who speaks first loses.*

"Okay. Do it"

Holy shit! Did I hear that right? I looked over at Tommy. Even though he was not on the phone, he was close enough that he could hear Dr. Ebert. He nodded yes.

"Okay, great!" I had learned to button up my trades to prevent reneges. "Here is what I'm going to do. At the open, we'll buy fifty thousand shares of MVSI at five dollars per share. It's a small trade. That's two hundred fifty thousand dollars due in five days. Thank you for the vote of confidence, Dr. Ebert. Let me go to work for you."

<hr />

And with that said, I hung up. *Oh my god.* Tommy came over and hugged me! We were hootin' and hollerin'! I had just raised a quarter of a million dollars with one trade! I brought in half of what Frankie was looking for, so I got ready to leave. Fuck it. They could unlock the goddamn door for me. Fuck 'em—I had just raised half of the money myself. I was entitled to go home and let the hundreds of other brokers in the room worry about the rest! With that done, I said good night to the midget, and went home.

Freddy had dinner waiting for me. I was so excited that I could hardly eat. We went into our tiny bedroom with its massive bed and made wild, passionate love until we were exhausted. When we were done, I crawled under the goose-down duvet and I fell unconscious, forgetting how angry I had been several days ago. *Money changes everything.* It was a good day.

I woke up at the crack of dawn, was really excited about the trade. If nothing else, I wanted to see the look on Roni's face when she heard about it. To my surprise, Frankie didn't make a big deal about it at the morning meeting, and Roni, as usual, was late for work and missed the entire meeting anyway. Whether it was intentional or not, I couldn't say for sure, though I had my suspicions.

Frankie looked at the ticket, very casually, and sniffed. "Nice trade."

I wanted to scream at him: *Nice trade? Are you fuckin' kidding me? I just raised a quarter of a million dollars, and that's all you have to say? Just in case you didn't hear that, I raised two hundred and fifty thousand dollars, a quarter of a million dollars, by myself!*

"Thanks, Frankie!" was all that I said.

I was that sure Roni had finally heard that I, rookie broker extraordinaire, had taken down a block of fifty. It was all that everyone in the boardroom was talking about, and it gave me a new title that I accepted with pride: I was now known as Ginger Big Blocks.

"*I am so fuckin' bad!* I'm a Stratton Oakmont broker!"

I quickly forgot the idea of leaving the family. I could taste the money and the power that would come with it. Anyway, I really liked this company whose stock I had bought for Dr. Ebert., and believed that my customers might finally actually have a chance to make money.

I felt like the *baddest* female broker in Lake Success. That weekend, I decided that I needed to drive a car that would show my successful career, not recognizing that with that decision I had become a willing victim, doing exactly what Stratton Oakmont wanted. I walked into the Ferrari showroom dressed in sweats. The snooty fuckers completely ignored me since I was not accompanied by a man. It didn't help that I was dressed like shit. The situation called for Ginger the Bitch to spring into action. I walked into the manager's tacky office and sat my butt down on his pleather sofa. The manager was a flash from the past, and his office was right out of the 1950s, with chrome everywhere. He even looked just like Elvis.

I whipped out a brown paper bag, looked him in the eye, and asked the price of the "cute little car in the showroom." He glared at me. "Do you know the one I'm talking about? The yellow one. It is *so* cute—mellow yellow."

I started SINGING: "*I'm just mad about Saffron*"

The manager rolled his eyes. "You might want to look next door." He meant the Volkswagen dealership. "They have a yellow car that might be a better fit for you." He meant cheaper. Apparently he was not a Donovan fan.

I looked at the manager and said. "You just made the biggest mistake of your life!" I left his office and asked the receptionist where I might find the owner of the dealership. When I was finally introduced to Jake Goodman, I said, "I want to buy that cute little yellow car in the showroom. And I would really appreciate it if you could ring me up."

Jake was obviously the owner of this dealership for a reason. I mean, come on, who walks into a Ferrari showroom and asks someone to ring them up? He did not act the least bit surprised.

"Are we looking at the yellow Testarossa?" he asked, stepping closer to it and running a hand along its smooth body. "Very hot car! You can drive this beauty out of here for a little over a hundred."

"I really wanted the car in red, to compliment my strawberry-blond hair, but when I saw the taxi cab yellow, it screamed my name Ginger. Ginger."

Jake Goodman thought that I had lost my mind. But I was having so much fun that I didn't care.

This car and I belonged together! Testarossa, Testa Rossa, TR—in Italian it meant red head. It was meant to be! Of course, Ferrari originally called it the Testa Rossa to refer to the Ferrari's red cylinder heads, but what did I know or care about that? I decided that the car was my destiny. I took the cash out of my brown paper bag and slowly counted it. It came to one hundred and one thousand dollars. We had a deal. This was going to be a great commuter car! It was only a twenty-minute ride to Stratton Oakmont from Port Washington, and I could not wait to let it loose on the quiet—at ten at night they were fairly empty—access roads. The international symbol of wealth and luxury seemed a fitting tribute to Ginger Big Blocks.

The roads into Port Washington were rarely deserted. However, during the crazy hours that I would drive to and from work they were pretty close to being deserted. I wanted to test out my new car. When I crossed over Northern Boulevard, I thought that I should see what the car had. There were only two or three traffic lights before I would hit that long stretch of road, which was one reason it was so safe in Port Washington. There was only one way in and one way out.

Let's see what this baby's got! I floored it. One hundred...one twenty...one forty...red flashing lights...shit! *Red flashing lights.* It *was* safe in Port Washington.

"Ginger Rogers? Is that you? It is! What the heck have you been up to?"

The police officer was a Persian dude that I knew from the Garment Center. I slowly eased myself out of the car, so that he would get a really nice look at my legs.

"Majid? What are you doing in that sexy uniform?" I tried to flirt with the hottie, but it was not working. I quickly realized that I had stiff competition: my Testarossa. I had to act fast. I sidled up to him as close as I could possibly get and I slipped him my business card. "Call me when you are off duty, and you can test drive it."

He said that he would. Then he warned me that the other officers would ticket me for sure. "Please be careful."

"Okay, Majid. Love ya!"

He never even mentioned that he must have clocked me going a hundred miles an hour over the limit! Oh, well!

I was not sure how much new money was raised in total the night that Frankie locked the brokers in the boardroom. However, an IPO was slated to open within the next few days, and I knew that I would raise additional funds. It was a company called Dual Star Technologies.ague It would not be a problem! Who could say no to Ginger Big Blocks?

I still needed to get the money in from Dr. Ebert for the fifty thousand shares of MVSI. I had some time, but the stock had slipped a quarter. Shit. Why now? I decided to place a call to Dr. Ebert to see if he had sent the payment and when. I needed the right amount of confidence to make the call and knew that if I sounded nervous, I could blow up the whole deal. I wasn't too worried. I had buttoned him up good. I finally got him on the phone. I could tell from his voice that he was not the least bit worried about sending a complete stranger a quarter of a million dollars. I could also tell that he was not a free rider and that he would definitely pay. When I reached him, after a few pleasantries I asked Dr. Ebert very casually if he had sent the payment.

He said that he had, seemingly quite proud of having done it himself. "I put it in the FedEx envelope and placed it in the mailbox myself." His pride deflated when he realized what he had just said. His usual polite reserve went out the window. "Oh, shit, Ginger! I dropped the FedEx package in the mailbox!"

It was a good thing that I had made that call. He overnighted me another check, and it actually made it to my desk on time. What a relief! However, I noticed that there was still one minor problem. Checks were never given directly to the broker unless there was a problem. I could not believe my eyes when I opened the package. Dr. Ebert had made the check out to me personally! I admit that the temptation to leave town was there, although how far would I get with only two hundred and fifty thousand dollars? No way. The real problem was that Stratton Oakmont had *not* totally corrupted me. I was not a thief! Rats.

"I'm not gonna lie to you; it did cross my mind," I told Freddy when I got home.

I could not figure out how Stratton Oakmont had been able to cash a check made out to me, but they had. They must have used a bank that *really* liked them, or one that followed the same code of ethics. I was asked to inform my customer that future trades should be paid with checks made out to Stratton Oakmont. Once again, I was the talk of the boardroom.

Although I was doing well at Stratton Oakmont, the come-to-Jesus meetings seemed to be happening on a much more frequent basis. When Frankie wasn't high, he might hold something that resembled a normal meeting—as if brainwashing could be considered normal. "At Stratton Oakmont, you have the ability to get rich. Liquid. How great would it feel to have a hundred thousand dollars in cash sitting in your bank account? We do the best deals. If you leave Stratton Oakmont, you will be out of the family and you will need to memorize the line 'Welcome to Wal-Mart.'"

The sarcastic sense of humor was prevalent throughout the boardroom, and no one was spared. When Glen Polansky wore an extremely loud Versace jacket one day, one of the brokers followed him around humming the tune for the Ringling Bros. and Barnum & Bailey Circus. Glen was so mad that he stopped and screamed at the broker, "This fuckin' jacket cost more than your car!"

One night when Frankie was lucid and in rare form, he told a story. "Last night I had dinner with a friend. Most of you guys are too young to remember this, but do any of you guys remember *The Honeymooners*, the show that starred Jackie Gleason? We were trying to remember the theme song. Does anyone remember how it goes?"

For some reason, he needed to know how that melody went. Frankie asked the room again. "Anyone here remember it?" Although everyone was really too young to remember that show, at some point in their lives they might have heard the theme song, and almost certainly had heard of Jackie Gleason. The next day, when the meeting was wrapping up, one of the brokers stood up with a trumpet and started playing "You're My Greatest Love," the theme to *The Honeymooners*. Everyone in the boardroom went wild.

Frankie always knew how to get everyone going and that day was no exception. "We're *bad*. We're *Stratton fuckin' Oakmont*. We do the best deals on the street! We help fund small companies and take them public. No one ever talks about that! Companies like Octagon Engineering, whose IPO went from seven to twenty-one the first day of trading. Steve Madden Shoes doubled in price. And this is another stock that every one of your customers should own: MVSI. I am telling you right now that there are *great* things going on with MVSI, things that I can't talk about because of the 'quiet period.' But I am telling you that the company is poised to be a hundred-million-dollar firm. You cannot buy enough of it at this level."

I always loved the quiet period bullshit. The quiet period or waiting period was a rule that I believed was an SEC rule. However, today's federal securities laws do not even define it! When a company went public, the quiet period was a time that the federal securities laws would limit the information that the company could release to the public. Disclosing new information on the company was prohibited. The quiet period extended from the time a company filed a registration statement with the SEC until the SEC staff declared that the registration statement "was effective." The rule, which dated back to the Securities Act of 1933, was apparently changed in 2005, by which point it had become obvious that the Internet would make it practically impossible to restrict all information. In the '90s it was a great bullshit line. Frankie used it constantly!

"I would LOVE to give you the details of this company, Mr. Customer, but you know that they are in the quiet period." My other favorite was the Chinese wall, which was a metaphorical barrier between different divisions of a financial institution to avoid conflicts of interest. It was another means of restricting the flow of information which was exactly what Frankie used it for, too.

I knew I was getting sucked into this world. It had become nearly impossible to turn it off outside of the office. One weekend, I ran into a former garmento colleague on the train to Manhattan.

"Ginger Rogers!" he said. "How *are* you, darling? How do you like working as a broker?"

"It's an absolutely incredible job. I am making *so* much money." I saw by the look on his face that my answer was boorish, and definitely not normal. It was more like the point of the end-of-the-month meetings when we were required to stand up and announce to the room how much we had grossed. Clearly, I was finding it more and more difficult to distinguish what was considered normal in the real world from typical Stratton Oakmont behavior.

I liked my new status and my new seat. I had learned several lessons sitting next to Tommy. Tommy was one of the more successful brokers at Stratton. He was a big guy, at least 6'2 and 220 pounds, with the sweetest baby face. He had a deep voice that intimidated his customers. And, as I found out when he helped me trade, he was probably the biggest ball grabber and scratcher in the firm. He really went to town down there when he was focused on trading.

I'd also learned that the brokers' success was directly related to how friendly they were with the principals of the firm, Josh, Glen, and Frankie. When I realized that if I had sucked Glen's dick I would have done twice the gross, the thought turned me off so much that I lost all interest in doing it!

A third lesson was that the big brokers did their gross by churning their accounts. When we had large positions it was easy to justify that. The fifty thousand shares of MVSI for Dr. Ebert fell into that category. The position could book a nice return if I could lock in a quarter point, assuming that I was allowed to sell it. Unfortunately, it was *such* a large position that I would need special approval to move in and out of it. Otherwise, I ran the risk of hurting the stock. That was how Stratton maintained prices and manipulated the market, as disclosed in the "welcome" documents that nobody read. Which brought me back to lesson number two: if we were friendly with the principals, we were allowed to sell. A fifty-thousand-share position would be hard to sell under most circumstances without significantly impacting the price of the stock.

The last lesson was that when all else failed, we should flip the customers into warrants! That was a great way to do gross. Warrants typically traded in tandem with the stock, and at a discount to the stock, so they were a very aggressive and, because they could expire, speculative way to increase a client's position—and our gross.

One of the last IPOs that I bought at Stratton was a company called Dual Star Technologies. It was the end of the day when the executives from Dual

Star had done their road show in front of the boardroom. The road show was a way of getting the brokers excited about a company so that they would recommend it to customers. They explained the company to the broker, what the company did, whether it was profitable or not, and their strategy for the future growth.

Dual Star Technologies Corporation operated as a holding company. Before the road show, Dual Star was described as an international company that designed and installed infrastructure systems and provided services that controlled the environment in buildings. In other words, they sold and installed boilers. That was why a road show was so important.

Brokers could sell a stock better if they understood what the business entailed. In some instances, like this one, it was probably better *not* to do a road show. Imagine a couple of maintenance men who happened to own a small company doing a dog-and-pony show for a bunch of wild animals. They were practically laughed out of the building.

To ensure the success of an IPO on its first day of trading, the brokers were told to get an indication of interests. Selling an IPO before it was available was illegal, so our workaround was to get dollar amount for the *probable* investments from customers. Most of the customers heard only what they wanted to hear ("our last IPO tripled the first day of trading") and failed to process what was actually said. "Mr. Jones, I'm going to give you as much IPO stock as I can. When the stock opens, we'll buy the balance. We'll try to fill it before it ticks higher." The average customer was given a hundred shares of IPO stock.

Stratton Oakmont had several other rules that the brokers had to follow regarding IPO stock. It could not be offered to a new account. No one wanted to sell stock to an IPO whore, and we would not make any friends if we were to unknowingly sell to one. More importantly, we would not make any money.

IPOs were to be divided by the size of the customer. Dr. Ebert would get the lion's share of my allocation. When we brought Dual Star public, one of my customers had given an indication of ten thousand dollars. I fully explained what I would invest his money in and I buttoned him up in my usual way. I told all my customers that I would buy100 shares of IPO stock (or whatever the amount was that they were getting)and then the balance of the funds would go toward aftermarket stock. I did not know where it would open but I would get it as close to the first tick as possible.

If a customer gave me an indication of interest of ten thousand dollars for both IPO units and after-market stock, they might end up with a portfolio of mostly common stock that was up or down. There was no way of predicting what would happen. With Octagon engineering, if you bought common stock at the open, you could have made money depending on the price that you paid and how long you held it. Freddy and I doubled our money and we did not even buy it as an IPO. With some of the other Companies that Stratton brought public, you lost money if you bought it the first day of trading. In this example, the after-market budget was the difference between the cost of the IPO units and ten thousand dollars. So the customer would have bought eighty-six hundred dollars. in aftermarket stock. One of the reasons that Stratton Oakmont's IPOs did so well was the way it was packaged. Customers saw the unit that. Stratton Oakmont typically offered as a good deal. They always offered IPOs as units, which seemed to be an attractive offer

The IPO stock was priced at seven dollars per unit—a unit typically consisted of two shares of common stock and two warrants—and the common stock was purchased at a slight premium. At the end of the day, it was no bargain. Customers looking to take their profit were talked out of it.

After reviewing the complaints against us I realized that I needed to move on immediately, if not sooner. My U4 debacle was certainly a wake-up call.

The roaches were starting to come out of the woodwork. The next ugly little bug that reared his head was Bernie Haven, a Southern black dude—in the '90s they were black, not African American—who had opened an account with me because he liked me. Maybe he was flattered that some crazy white woman even talked to him. Stratton Oakmont's attorney would later tell me that she was amazed at how he had flirted with me when I first pitched him. When Roni got through with him, though, he was as bitter as a jilted lover. He never liked her, and his feelings were hurt when I passed him over to Roni. Bernie lost a small amount of money on one stock and actually made money on another, but he felt spurned.

I could tell that Bernie was divorced—who would put up with his shit? It was obvious from the way he acted when he lost money. HE was a geek who loved electronics, and that the most exciting event in his recent life was opening an account with Ginger Rogers. Bernie, to his credit, did do his homework on Stratton Oakmont. There were so many lawsuits at this time that Bernie wanted some of that action. Of course, the lawsuits that made the news were the ones where the poor investors won big settlements.

I was upset when Bernie sent in his letter claiming failure to sell stock. When I read the actual complaint, though, I had to laugh. It may sound like I was a heartless bitch, but really, come on, who writes a letter complaining that their broker made them impotent? The new joke around Stratton Oakmont was, "Watch out for Ginger Big Blocks! She'll make your dick limp!"

Frankie loved that type of battle. "Come on, Ginger! You tell that motherfucker to bring it on! He wants to sue me? You tell that rat bastard that he needs to get in line!"

It may have been fine for Frankie to talk tough and invite a fight, but it was tough for most of the rest of the brokers. Frankie was rich...and insane. He was getting worse every day. He seemed oblivious to the concept of jail time. Did he care if he went to jail? I didn't think so. Frankie had the money to hire the best attorneys in the country. I did not.

Bernie had obviously read about several lawsuits and the cash settlements that former Stratton Oakmont customers were getting. But he most likely read about another trial that had nothing to do with Stratton Oakmont. In 1995, many Americans were obsessed with the O. J. Simpson trial. I am quite sure that Bernie studied the trial in depth, since he used a defense that I named "The O. J. Simpson defensive maneuver." Simpson had been accused of brutally murdering his ex-wife, Nicole Brown Simpson, and her boyfriend, Ronald Goldman. It didn't matter that shoe prints from a size twelve Bruno Magli shoe were found at the crime scene and in Simpson's car and that Simpson wore a size twelve shoe and had been photographed wearing Bruno Magli shoes. Simpson maintained his innocence by stating over and over again that it wasn't him. "I know you have pictures of me wearing Bruno Magli shoes, but it wasn't me." The O. J. Simpson defensive maneuver. It reminded me of advice that I had been given by a friend "I don't care if you get caught with your hand in the register. What you say is "It wasn't me" Classic defensive maneuver.

Bernie claimed that Roni Van Brunt failed to sell his stock as he had requested. Roni and I knew that he was lying. We had both spoken to him several times during that period, and not once had he asked either Roni or me to sell his stock. In addition to our testimony, we had Stratton pull the recorded conversations, and those supported our assertions that he never asked Roni to sell the stock in question. This is where he used the O. J. Simpson defensive maneuver: "I know that both Roni Van Brunt and Ginger Rogers claim that I never asked them to sell my stocks, and the tapes do not show that I asked them to sell, but I asked them to sell."

It was pure O. J. Simpson. He had studied his lines.

On October 2, 1995, the Simpson jury announced that they had reached a verdict. After fewer than four hours of deliberation, they had found him not guilty. I was in the boardroom when the verdict came in. It was one of the most divisive events of the '90s. Lines were drawn and divided by race. Blacks tended to swear he was innocent and a victim of white privilege and discrimination who had been framed. Whites tended to insist that he was guilty. Some people called it the "trial of the century," and it did have a lot of high-profile dramatic appeal, which turned it into a media circus. Simpson, a Heisman trophy winner, was wealthy and good looking. Even the judge presiding over the case, Lance Ito, was star struck, which may be one reason that the case dragged on for more than a year and stayed in the public eye like a bad reality-TV show. It was extremely popular conversational fodder around Stratton Oakmont in '94 and '95, so when the verdict finally came in, the boardroom—whose makeup was 99.9 percent white men—was almost dead silent in stunned disbelief. That was followed by sobs and cries of absolute disgust, with people asking what kind of a legal system would relentlessly pursue a firm like Stratton Oakmont for using sales scripts, yet was unable to prove beyond a reasonable doubt that the man was a cold-blooded murderer who had for years abused, terrorized, and eventually stabbed his ex-wife to death?

Bernie had obviously studied this case.

I know the tapes seem to prove that I never asked you to sell, but tapes can easily be edited.

Classic O. J. Simpson.

I wanted to fight the son of a bitch. He was a liar. We had done nothing wrong. But Stratton Oakmont had bigger fish to fry. Their position was that they would pay to get rid of the little roaches. I was sure that Bernie understood the firm's unspoken policy. The case ended up in mediation in Atlanta, where I had to try to be civil to that piece of shit. All I really wanted to do was spit in his face. We were forced to settle, and. Bernie walked away with a nice check for twenty thousand dollars. The mediation agreement also required both Roni and me to sign a form stating that we neither admitted to, nor denied, any wrongdoing.

Wow. No big deal, right? Then I found out that my license had been suspended in Georgia and half dozen other states for two years. I wondered how it could be that this assumption of guilt was not a violation of the laws in America. Shouldn't the suspensions have been mentioned before I signed? I had existing customers in some of those states! It was unbelievable. All because of that lying piece of shit. I should never have stayed at Stratton Oakmontas long as I did.

I was so disgusted that when I received a call from the SEC guys that I had met with so many months before, I was intrigued. I was also not surprised. This was my wake-up call, courtesy of good old Frick and Frack.

"Ginger Rogers, please."

"This is Ginger. Who's this?"

"Hi, Ginger. I don't know if you remember me, but we met about a year ago at Stratton Oakmont. This is William Frick from the SEC."

I was truly caught off guard. "How are you, Mr. Frick?"

"I'm fine, but I'm worried about you!"

"Really? Why is that?

"I'm worried because you're still working at Stratton Oakmont," he said. He wasn't laughing. He was serious. "Ginger, you need to get out of there. You need to go *now*!"

"I know. But I'm trapped. I had a partnership with another broker and they put her complaints on my U4," I said. "Prudential offered me a position. When they saw my U4, they rescinded the offer."

"Well, then, maybe it's time to think about a career change," he said. "You need to get out now, before it's too late!"

I had always thought that I had made a good impression on them, and this phone call confirmed that.

"The Feds want Frankie in a big way," he said. "If they happen to call you, try not to worry. We put in a good word for you."

Yeah, right. I thought I understood the call. They were asking me to rat out my family. How could I do that? Although I knew in my heart that they were right: it was time to move on. Frankie was spinning out of control, and I did not want to go down with a sinking ship. I decided to put a major effort into finding another job.

Frankie spent a lot of time talking about his obsessions. He was completely obsessed with the author Sun Tzu and his wonderful book *The Art of War*, considered by many to be the ultimate sales bible. Even people who have not heard of the obscure author have heard him quoted often, probably without knowing it: "Can you imagine what I would do if I could do all I can?" What made his writing especially compelling was that Sun Tzu wrote these words in 6 BCE.

Probably the best-known quote attributed to Sun Tzu was "Keep your friends close, and your enemies closer," and although I'd been told that it was really a line from *The Godfather: Part II*—What else?—that sounded similar to something that Sun Tzu had been known to say, it didn't matter because it was one of Frankie's favorite sayings. He even had it tacked up on his office wall: *Keep your friends close, and your enemies closer.*

Frankie would get wasted and sit in his office reading Sun Tzu and watching movies like *The Godfather*, *GoodFellas*, and *Scarface* over and over again. It was weird. *He* was weird—and getting weirder. In the summer of 1995, Frankie threw a party at Jared Bellmore's place in the Hamptons. Freddy and I decided to go, along with Sal and his wife. We were planning on staying at Sal's house after the party; Sal lived in one of those miserable Suffolk county towns that was close to the Hamptons, but not *in* the Hamptons, and far from every other place that most people might want to go. I guess technically it was not really far, but considering the traffic at any given moment on the Long Island Expressway—The World's Biggest Parking Lot—it was far. Ask Long Islanders how far away a destination is, and they won't answer in terms of mileage but in terms of time, and how long it will take given the route.

We got to Sal's house at six o'clock and I knew right away what to expect. Sal had often complained to me about his crazy neighbor. When Freddy and I pulled up at Sal's house, I noticed his neighbor's manicured lawn and immaculate grounds. Sal's house had several abandoned cars parked in the driveway, Christmas decorations that he had never bothered to remove from the yard even though it was June, and grass that must have been knee-high.

Sal answered the door. His house was a once-white '70s-style ranch that was an even bigger mess on the inside than on the outside, which I hadn't thought possible.

"Ginger! How are ya, baby? Come on in. Did you guys find this place okay?"

"Oh, yeah. Piece of cake."

"Hey, let me show you around. Here's where you guys will be sleeping."

I muttered something to the effect that his house was quite *charming* and *unique*. Meanwhile, the musty smell that met us at the front door solidified my feeling that there was no way I was sleeping there that night. Freddy looked at my face and knew.

"Where are your bags?"

"Unfortunately, it turns out that Ginger and I need to get back to Port Washington tonight. Our babysitter cancelled, and we have to pick Brian up at Ginger's mom's house."

So, we made our excuses in advance and proceeded to the party. That was okay. I really wanted to fuck my husband that night at home in our own bed! I was not sure what was going on with him—with us. Lately Freddy was never home, and we had not had sex in months. I would not have felt comfortable having sex in Sal's house and was thrilled that Freddy could see that.

When we finally made it to West Hampton, the party was already out of control. The back yard and was packed with people. I was very happy that we had decided to take our car, even though parking was really a problem; most neighborhoods in West Hampton do not allow parking on the street. Freddy, however, was very resourceful when it came to parking, and managed to find a spot on the large circular driveway.

Finally, Frankie showed his face and began to give the crowd his Stratton Oakmont speech. Jared Bellmore's house in West Hampton was a large, white contemporary monstrosity. There was a nice pool in the back and a balcony that overlooked it, probably the master bedroom. Since we were not allowed inside, I could not confirm that. Frankie was wasted on Quaaludes and could barely talk. I suddenly realized that I was so done with that scene that I wasn't even sure why we were there. I tried to totally tune Frankie out that night, although I can remember him starting his chanting frenzy: *Work hard, play hard. Work hard, play hard, Work hard, play hard! We are Stratton fuckin' Oakmont! Stratton fuckin' Oakmont! Stratton fuckin' Oakmont!*

It was the worst that I had ever seen Frankie.

I decided we had to leave when I saw that Frankie was standing on the second-floor balcony, shouting at the crowd. He was very close to the rail, and so out of control that I was afraid that the next sound that I would hear would be a thump-splat. I suspected that his capos were also concerned, as they flanked him closely, and were holding his arms when we left. I was certain that the night would not end well.

Freddy managed to get me home in one piece, but as usual he said he was too tired to have sex. I smiled sadly to myself. Wasn't it the woman who supposedly said that?

When I returned to work on Monday, I knew that it was the end of my time at Stratton Oakmont. The final impetus had been a phone call I had received the night before.

"Hello? Yes, this is Ginger. Who is this?"

"My name is James Blackstone. I got your name from Mr. Frick at the SEC. He spoke very highly of you, by the way. He said you are a woman with integrity."

Oh? Well, that was certainly nice of him.

"Ginger, I'm sorry to trouble you at home, but I didn't want to call you at Stratton Oakmont. I'm with the FBI," said Blackstone. "There are a number of bad brokers there that need to be taken out of the system. We have evidence, but we are asking a number of people, including you, to cooperate with us and testify against them." Testify? Leaving Stratton Oakmont was one thing, but he was asking me to rat out the family. I didn't think I could do it.

"Working with the FBI...that makes it sound dangerous," I said. "I have a family to think about, you know." Two of them, actually. The principals were all obsessed with organized crime,

but I had always figured that they had no connections to the real family, just fantasies. Now I wondered.

"Initially your role would be anonymous. If it comes to open testimony, you would be disguised so that you are unrecognizable and you will have the full protection of the Federal Bureau of Investigation. Worst case, of course, there's witness protection, but I don't see it ever coming to that."

"I need to think about it."

"Of course. Think it over, Ginger. I'll call you in two weeks."

Even Glen had let me down. He was having an affair with a new, younger, and prettier version of me. How could I compete? I felt so inferior and so let down. At least I had one big thing going for me that she did not. Or, rather, two big things: tits. Mine were huge. She was as flat as my ironing board. *Never heard of implants, bitch?*

So it was that on that beautiful March morning, I walked into Glen's office and gave him my letter of resignation. He must have been fine with it, as he didn't say a word, almost as though he had been expecting it. He would have been, of course. Glen Polansky would be able to figure out that anyone with half a brain wouldn't want to stay there long, especially now that rumors were flying that key people associated with the firm were about to be arrested, fined, and censured, and the firm shut down. I knew it, and Glen knew it too, but like the captain going down with the ship, he would stay to the bitter end.

I had recently interviewed at a boutique brokerage house in Manhattan called Bishop Allen. Although I had my reservations about the owner, Sam Shulman, he had an impressive résumé, so over the weekend I had I decided that I would accept his offer. My main concern was that although he had seemed open and forthcoming, making good eye contact throughout the interview, when I had asked him about liquidity I thought I detected a change. He looked away from me as he answered that yes, I would have liquidity, and after that, his answers seemed more guarded, even scripted. It should have reminded me of recent experiences, but I had always had a fairly active imagination that needed to be tempered, at times, with a strong dose of common sense. So I just told myself to forget about it. Why would he lie to me? He was a licensed securities rep, and the owner of the firm!

Grow up, sister! Will you ever learn?

Well, I hadn't learned yet. I had left the interview really believing that I could make money for myself at Bishop Allen and, equally important, that I could make money for my customers. I didn't recognize, or chose to ignore, warning signs that it was not going to be an improvement over Stratton Oakmont.

A week later, in April of 1996, I reported for work at the office of Bishop Allen on 40 Broad Street. It was unbearably hot and humid in New York that day. It seemed more like summer than the beginning of April. I thought of Glen Polansky when I arrived at the office dripping wet with sweat. I needed an office with a change of clothes! The office was located right on Broad Street next door to the New York Stock Exchange, on the corner of Broad and Wall. Wall Street. It is really the place where it was all happening. And I loved working downtown, which was something new to me after spending so many years in midtown Manhattan in the Garment Center. Downtown, I would be surrounded by the corporate headquarters of most of the city's financial institutions, including the Federal Reserve. I would also be within walking distance of the World Trade Center, which I could never look at without thinking of Bill Levine.

I hoped that would change, because I had always thought of the Twin Towers as being one of the more glamorous buildings in New York. Perhaps that was because I had been mesmerized by the video of acrobat Philippe Petit dancing back and forth on his tightrope between the towers, a quarter of a mile above the ground. Maybe I loved it there because of the abundance of luxury stores that were located below ground! I liked to take long walks after the market closed for the day, walking by my favorite buildings, spending hours just window shopping along with the thousands of people that traversed the area on a daily basis.

From the day they were completed, the Twin Towers were criticized as architectural obscenities. To the architectural world, they were ugly, boxy structures. I never thought of them that way, though, and didn't care what others thought: to me, they were a proud symbol of Manhattan and everything that I loved about living there. When I was lost, they guided me. When I was upset, I found comfort in visiting them. When I felt restless, their incredible views calmed me. When they were gone, I believe a part of me went missing, too.

Downtown was an amazing place to work! Several of the cobblestone streets in the financial area were open only to pedestrian traffic, which I found to be a wonderful and a completely foreign experience for me. It seemed that there was one festival or another happening there every night, which made me feel as though I was working all over the world—Paris one day, Rome the next—and it was perfect. Well, it was almost perfect.

I had managed to get all of my clients out of Stratton Oakmont and over to Bishop Allen. I was so relieved to be out of Stratton Oakmont that I did not see what was happening at Bishop Allen, thought that it was going well until one day I received a call from a client.

"Hello, Ginger. This is Barry Jones."

"How are ya, Barry?"

"I was great until I got my latest statement. Then I saw that not only am I down on *every* position but the five thousand shares of Sel-Leb Marketing are *still* sitting in my account. Can you please explain why?"

"No, that must be a mistake. I placed a sell for you right after we spoke," I said. "Let me look into it and call you right back."

When I "looked into" the situation, I was very upset to find out that the stock had not been sold and was, as Barry had said, still sitting in his account. Today, nearly everything is handled electronically, but in 1995, the process was still almost entirely manual. I would hand-write a paper ticket and walk it over to the trading desk. If the trading desk was far away from your workspace, if the stock was running you could easily pay up a quarter or a half by the time you bought it. I heard one of the brokers explain it to a customer.

"Do you watch *Seinfeld*? This is like that scene when Jerry wants to buy a chocolate babka. He walks into the bakery and *sees* the babka. He *wants* the babka. But when he gets to the counter, the babka is *gone!*"

Bishop Allen wanted me to think that somewhere between my client's request to sell the stock, and my delivery of the paper ticket to the trading window, someone had eaten Barry's babka. But what really happened is that someone had taken my sell ticket and ripped it up. They *ripped* it up!

I started to grow suspicious, and soon learned that it was all true: Sam *had* lied to me that first day, and I was investing in illiquid garbage—again—at another roach motel. Ignoring a sell request is the kind of shit that lands brokers in jail, so once again I knew that it was time to get the fuck out of there! Sam was no better than Frankie. In fact, I recalled wondering about Sam when he mentioned that the traders at Stratton Oakmont were looking for MVSI, and knew that I had a block of it, since Dr. Ebert's fifty thousand shares had moved with me from Stratton Oakmont. That did not seem kosher to me, him knowing what Stratton Oakmont wanted. It was kind of like tipping your hand in poker.

Yet I had started at Bishop Allen with such great hope! I was even a principal—sort of, anyway: Sam had asked me to take the Series 24 exam so I could manage some of the new recruits, and I now had my "principal" license. It hadn't, however, changed my status, compensation, or knowledge of Bishop Allen's internal affairs. Had I really been a principal, I would have known about Bishop Allen's connection to Vinny Ke, understood the whole sordid big picture, and run like hell. Soon after I had joined Stratton Oakmont, I heard whispers about someone named Vinny Ke who somehow had links to the firm. I had completely forgotten about him until I started at Bishop Allen. Vinny had once been CEO of of a company called Judicate Inc., They were a firm that specialized in alternative dispute resolution that had been taken public by Stratton. In 1993, Vinny had started a brokerage firm called Duke Securities that had an office in midtown Manhattan and one on Long Island.

I remembered having heard Frankie rant about someone named Ke during several meetings, cursing him loudly. Frankie despised Vinny, probably because his rival Duke was a force to be reckoned with. The firm had about thirty-five thousand customer accounts whose combined investments with Duke were somewhere in the neighborhood of $171 million. The firm's reputation wasn't great, however. (By the time it was closed by the feds in March of 1998, it would be the subject of twenty-six regulatory actions.)What a surprise. That should have made Frankie happy, but he didn't have a good word to say about the man or about Duke. I didn't know what Frankie's problem with Vinny was, but I figured it was just him picking at some old scab, repeating himself. He did that a lot.

A month or two after I had started at Stratton Oakmont, before I really new much more about the place than how to hear the phrase "piker midget asshole" without laughing, one of the more veteran brokers had quit in a fury. While he was being escorted out by a red-faced Frankie, he had shouted that "Stratton Oakmont is nothing but a roach motel!" (the first time I'd heard the term, and that made me laugh, too—back then) and a few moments later that "the game was rigged."

"This damned nuthouse is bankrolling the Crazy Chinaman!" I had no clue what he was talking about at the time.

So, somewhere in the back of my mind, I had remembered that that Duke was a roach motel that was created as a clone of Stratton Oakmont. Duke Securities was run by Vinny Ke in the exact same way that Stratton was run. They even did their own IPOs. IT was obvious that Frankie detested him and trashed him at every opportunity. After I became a broker and privy to a few more...*interesting*...conversations (okay, I eavesdropped on the principals now and then), I learned that Vinny was Vinny Ke—also known as the Crazy Chinaman. So I had figured out that three of the enemies were really the same person. I was one puzzle piece closer to seeing the big picture.

Recently I had learned that a lot of the Bishop Allen brokers had previously worked for Duke Securities. Sam Shulman himself had mentioned one day that he had spent the weekend on his friend Vinny's yacht. And now Sam had let it slip that he communicated with people at Stratton Oakmont. What was going on here? One of the reasons that I worked at Bishop Allen was to get away from Strattton Oakmont. It never occurred to me to ask where the funding came from and had I asked, I would not have believed the answer. It took many years to get that last piece of the puzzle. But I finally figured it out. Duke Securities was created and bankrolled by Jared Bellmore.

Oh. My. God. It was like a fuckin' roach motel FRANCHISE operation. The nuthouse funding Duke—Vinny KE, the Crazy Chinaman—was Stratton Oakmont. It made sense when I really thought about it. It was Sun Tzu at his best. "Keep your friends close, and your enemies closer". If they funded The Chinaman's operation, they would know exactly what he was up to, a pure Frankie move.

So I had I basically just added an hour to my morning commute. I was still working for Stratton Oakmont! I now understood why Glen hadn't seemed at all surprised when I resigned to take the job at Bishop Allen. He had already known that I had accepted the job.

I was livid. I marched down to Sam's office, screaming so loudly that I can't believe the police didn't show up, "You *motherfuckers!* You fuckin' *lied* to me! How *dare* you rip up my sell ticket! I will have you all *arrested*, you lying, cheating bastards!"

I was not sure how but I would get them, but I would make it my mission to get not just Sam Shulman but the whole damn bunch of rotten apples on the family tree. I stomped to my desk to grab my purse, but Sam got there first and threw it at me, blocking my way to my client book. I tried to push past, but Sam threatened me: "Ginger Rogers, if you touch one fuckin' thing on that desk, I will have you arrested for grand larceny."

Two beefy goons materialized. At Sam's nod, each one linked an arm through one of mine and half-escorted, half-carried me toward the door. I was still screaming. "You little *fucker!* Do you really believe that's is my only copy? I'll get you, Sam, I will. And by the way, the next time there's a knock on your door, I suggest you run."

"Do you think I'm afraid of you, you bitch? That's very funny."

"Oh, it won't be me. It will be a guy in a dark suit holding an ID with the initials FBI. And trust me, those initials don't stand for Fuckin' Bitches Incorporated."

I decided to give this broker thing one last shot. moved to HJ Meyers. Some of my clients moved with me, some chose to stay behind. And several I gave to my friend Patricia Dubois because my license was still suspended in that state. I was shocked to learn that Sam Shulman had flown to California to convince Dr. Ebert to keep his account with Bishop Allen, but I knew that I would eventually convince him to come with me, so I wasn't worried.

I really believed that I had found everything that I was looking for in HJ Meyers. They had fourteen offices, did deals that were liquid (initially), and were managed like a small firm. Once again, things started to spin out of control. When you are harassed by the geeks in IT, it's time to move on.

Patricia and I were the only two female brokers at HJ Meyers. We wanted to move our desks so that we could share a Quotron and, okay, be closer to our *hot, hot, hot* manager named Devin. The process required assistance from the IT guy. He set up the Quotron and told us that our access was granted. I had only spoken to him once before, in passing, so I was completely caught off guard when I asked him for my password and he said, with a smirk, BITCH_2. I could not believe the nerve of the guy. Patricia called the help desk and spoke to the resident geek, whom I had never met and had spoken with only twice. The geek informed Patricia that my password had been set and determined by the clearing agent, Cowen and Company, and could not be changed for a month.

We held our ground. I refused to use my password. We were going to forget about it and move on, but then we had drinks with a broker friend from Smith Barney who told us all about the infamous Boom-Boom Room and how she and the other women there were routinely humiliated, denied promotions, and called despicable names. When we told her about BITCH_2, she said, "Stand up for yourselves and do something now, or it will only get worse. If we just keep putting up with these macho jerks and their abusive, sexist bullshit, how will they ever learn that they have to take us seriously?"

She had a point. So when we returned to the office, Patricia started typing a complaint on the computer, only to have the screen freeze. New words magically appeared on the screen, sent by the geek: "Like I said, Patricia, Ginger's BITCH_2 password can't be changed for a month. But I could change YOUR password, so I did. Go ahead and send your complaint."

Great. The macho jerks could control our computers at will.

Further infuriated, Patricia finished typing the complaint and fired it off to management. We got no response. None. Not only that, the geek didn't tell Patricia what her new password was, so she was forced to make the trek to IT to find out. Fifteen minutes later she returned, slumped in her chair, and tossed an index card to me.

"My password," she said, looking resigned.

I read it. It said SLUT.

After working at HJ Meyers for a month, I finally felt like a real broker. I could buy and *sell* what I wanted, when I wanted. I was just settling in when I got a call—December 5, 1996—from Sal Angelli. Since I hadn't spoken to Sal in about six months, I knew it couldn't be good news.

Sal told me that the Feds had finally done it. They had finally shut down Stratton Oakmont. In a way, it was very sad, and felt a little tearful. It was the end of an era, and the end of my family. Yes, they were corrupt, insane, thieving assholes, but they were my corrupt, insane, thieving assholes! I decided that theirs was a story that needed to be told, and the notes that I took when I was working there have stayed with me until now. I felt sorry for everyone that remained at Stratton until the end, especially the customers. I saw on the news that Jared, over the course of several months, had sunk his 175-foot yacht, crashed his helicopter, and drove through his garage door, having forgotten to open it. In every case, Jared, who was in a downward spiral, had been so wasted that he couldn't make rational decisions.

When I thought about it, the guys at Stratton Oakmont had not been so bad. Then I got a call from Frick and Frack, and that changed everything. My old nemesis Bernie Haven was at it again. Not content with the paltry twenty-grand settlement that Stratton Oakmont had given him, Bernie had gone to the Feds. My SEC buddies were calling to tell me that the FBI would be calling me.

I thought about what I would say to the strangely creepy agent. I practiced my rebuttals. When James Blackstone finally called, I was unprepared for what he would say. Bernie had taken his sad tale of baseless price projections, unauthorized trading, and failure to sell to the FBI thinking that he should have aimed higher in the first place. Of course, this was not the complaint he had made before; Bernie had added additional charges.

It had apparently been so easy to get that first twenty thousand that he had decided to go for more, and to get it fast before they went under! He had obviously read about another lawsuit against Stratton Oakmont, and co-opted those allegations, knowing that those charges had won the largest punitive judgment ever for a customer in securities arbitration. Although it was doubtful that the customer ever collected anything, he had been awarded $10 million in punitive damages. In a very unusual move, the NASD panel had said that the punitive damages were to be paid by four Stratton officials, two of whom had had no direct contact with the customer, based on "their participation in the overall business of Stratton Oakmont." That did not sound right. Where was the assumption of innocence? Could that happen in a real court?

I could picture Bernie reading the complaints and deciding to use them as his own.

They were, without a doubt, Blackstone's hot buttons. If that were not bad enough, it seemed that the ever-so-charming Roni Van Brunt had thrown me under the bus to avoid going to jail. Roni had told the FBI that Bernie was my customer, and that she had very little to do with him! She had the nerve to tell Blackstone that she had only been required to go to the arbitration in Atlanta because she and I had a joint U4.

Blackstone, who was no dummy, thought that he should hear my side of the story. After all, Roni Van Brunt still worked at Stratton Oakmont, and I did not. Even today, I ask myself why I *ever* worked there, and the answer I always end up with is not surprising. I will always think of it as the best and worst job I ever had. I did it for the convenience: it was twenty minutes from home. I did it for the excitement: when stocks were running, whether it was up or down, we couldn't buy or sell them fast enough. I did it for the money: where else could a woman make that much money on Long Island? But most of all, I did it for the fame. The applause. The rush of earning my stripes, and becoming Ginger Big Blocks.

Unfortunately, in this case, Stratton Oakmont will always be remembered not for the small companies that the firm helped grow, like Steve Madden, which today has revenue of $288 million, but for all the investors that complained that they had been conned.

Was Stratton Oakmont a bad firm? The owners did operate on pure greed.

Was it unique? Hardly.

The years that I worked there as a broker taught me one thing: the little guys have to be very lucky to make money in the stock market. After leaving Stratton Oakmont, I opened personal brokerage accounts with firms like Morgan Stanley, Dean Witter, and Smith Barney, and they were all the same. Although they were finely polished gems, their brokers were no better than the ones at Stratton Oakmont. After working with several traditional firms as a private investor, I was shocked to learn that every firm had issues:

- UBS, the enormous Swiss bank, agreed to buy back $19.4 billion of failed auction-rate securities and pay a $150 million fine, the largest settlement in a US investigation into whether banks stuck clients with hard-to-sell bonds.
- Prudential Bache was sued by attorneys representing more than seven hundred investors who were pursuing limited-partnership claims against Prudential; the attorneys recovered more than $40 million on behalf of those investors.
- Bear Stearns agreed to a $250 million settlement over allegations that the brokerage facilitated improper trading in mutual funds.
- Merrill Lynch and Smith Barney were both sued in Boom-Boom Room discrimination cases.
- Merrill Lynch promoted sales of Enron stock even while the company was misstating its income and debt.
- Citigroup acquired detailed knowledge and insight of Enron's finances as lenders and vendors of financial services.
- UBS PaineWebber fired Chung Wu, the broker who was e-mailing clients, advising them to sell their Enron shares.

And these sanctions were against the so-called legitimate firms! What is a small investor to do? Blackstone's position on this was that no respectable firm would cram hundreds of young men—he had not heard of me, Ginger Rogers, at that point—into a big room to make hundreds of calls a day, using scripts, and high-pressure sales tactics.

As many former brokers do, I decided to leave New York. Freddy and I moved to our dream house in Boca Raton, Florida. South Florida's appeal is significantly more than the warm climate. The state's generous property laws make it a popular destination for boiler-room millionaires. The state makes then feel right at home. Florida's constitution protects a home of almost any value from being taken through the courts, and certain investments are shielded from creditors in bankruptcy proceedings. Boca Raton is considered to be a wonderful place for wealthy criminals. Most of the former Stratton Oakmont brokers ended up living like royalty in sunny Florida despite having been inundated with dozens of lawsuits.

It was in Boca, living in my McMansion, that my life finally fell apart. The little sex that Freddy and I still had became even less frequent in this new environment. I started a handbag company, and Freddy played tennis. And he played tennis. And he played tennis. I began to question moving to Florida, my life in general, and my love for Freddy. I had thought that we were happy together. He thought that we fought all the time. From the day that we arrived in Boca, I began *my* downward spiral.

I became suspicious of Freddy. Something was up. Why was he never home? And why was he always on his cell phone? Although I considered myself to be "technology challenged," I could navigate the web, which was how I found Cheaters.com. I read the tell-tale signs of a cheater and realized it sounded just like my husband: he was never home; he took his cell phone everywhere; he lost twenty pounds and bought all new clothes, for which I paid; and on and on and on.

His phone would ring at night around ten or ten-thirty—not very late, but much later than most of our friends would call. Freddy fell asleep early one night, and I grabbed his phone, determined to find out who it was. I didn't know how to send a text, but I knew how to read one. It was nothing earth shattering but I knew what it meant and I was devastated. The message said, "I thought you said you'd call me."

I confronted Freddy, who denied everything, but I needed the truth. In spite of my lack of knowledge, I transformed myself into Ginger Rogers, master hacker. I started with his cell phone. I discovered that AT&T should be called the Cheater's Friend, as it was next to impossible to hack into, with two layers of security before I could even get to the account data. I figured out his password for the first layer, then managed to get customer service to "remind me" of the second one.

Once I was in, I couldn't believe what I saw. Freddy was sending love notes, or what I assumed were love notes, to a woman in Daytona Beach. Dozens of notes. He seemed to spend every available opportunity texting her! I was stunned. Where had I been when this was taking place? In the bathroom? Getting dressed? How had I not caught on before?

I checked his phone bill. The affair had been going on for seven months. I was heart-broken. How could this have happened to us? We were once so in love.

Freddy denied everything. He insisted that they were "just friends." He must have thought that I was an idiot! Women do not call their "friends" twenty times a day.

I was unable to access Freddy's home email account at first. I had never bothered reading his email before, and was amazed at how easy it was to hack into. There it was in black and white: Her name was Lisa, the fuckin' bitch, and they both professed their undying love for each other.

Not happy at all, I decided to approach matters with my usual take-control style: I called the bitch.

Lisa answered the phone and I went into attack mode with full guns blazing.

"Is Freddy there?"

"Freddy? Freddy who?"

"Freddy Rogers. Is this Lisa?"

"Who is this?"

"This is Freddy's wife, Ginger. I know that you have been seeing him and since he is not home, I assumed that he was with you." I went on and on. "What kind of a woman are you, anyway, to break up a family? How do you live with yourself?"

Lisa was very quiet and then finally spoke up. "He told me he was divorced."

Divorced? Well, one of us was pretty stupid. I continued my attack. "You 'dated' him for seven months and never met his son? Never met his friends? Never went to his house? Or maybe I am wrong about that. Did you ever go to our house?"

"No, never."

"Yet you believed that he was divorced?"

Lisa assured me that from that moment on, Fredrick Rogers was out of her life.

But later I wondered why I had fought so hard for such a small victory when lately Freddy had been nothing but miserable with me, and I wasn't even sure why, or if, I loved him.

Maybe if I focused on my business, things would get better, but that seemed to be a no-win situation. When I was a broker, I had always tried to treat my customers fairly. I tried to make them money. I couldn't understand why, in the bull market of the '90s, when *everything* went up, I was still unable to pick stocks that didn't fall.

Now I felt just as stalled with my business in Boca, because it was hard to focus on what was happening at my business when I was so worried about what was going on at home.

Lisa kept her word, I believe, and never saw Freddy again. But I soon learned that if it wasn't Lisa, it was Paula…or Inez…or Teresa…or Ellie. Eventually I had to face the facts of life, and acknowledge my failed marriage and my second failed career. I had given my heart to Freddy and Stratton Oakmont, and they had both screwed me. I couldn't stay in a relationship like that, so eventually I divorced them both: the pump-and-dump roach motel, and the man who would hump-and-bump at any old motel. I was certain that they would both get what they deserved.

Several years after Stratton Oakmont was closed, I heard from James Blackstone. The Feds finally had enough evidence to convict thirty-three of the former Stratton Oakmont brokers; no, I was not one of them. I really believe I did nothing wrong.

Even though Blackstone had grown quite fond of me, and maybe because he did share Frick and Frack's opinion that I had integrity, he had to ask. "Ginger, I think you can now see them for what they are—nothing more than common thieves," he said. "You could have done jail time for that stunt they pulled at Bishop Allen. You're lucky that in spite of it all, that your customers really liked you. I know that in the past you were afraid to testify, but will you please reconsider your decision? I can assure you that you will have the full protection of the United States government and the FBI."

How could I testify against the family? I was stunned. How could Blackstone even *think* that I might consider turning against them? But he was persistent. Blackstone was finally able to convince me that with the FBI-provided disguise, I would be unrecognizable. He also let it slip that Jared Bellmore had given up Frankie, Glen, *and* Josh. They were *all* going to jail. It was on that same day in March that I found out that Freddy, who had moved out two years earlier and was working in the Garment Center, wanted to come back into my life. It was all starting to fall into place.

I finally agreed to testify. I took the stand wearing a brunette wig, fake nose, and glasses. Blackstone provided a voice-changing device. Even I didn't recognize me.

IT was several years later that I looked up my, my old friend Neil Hautz, now Dr. Hautz, who had recently transferred to Boca to become an assistant medical examiner. Neil had gone to medical school after college and had been sidetracked by an extremely attractive job offer in the garment center. It's funny how money changes everything.

I was looking forward to seeing Neil and catching up. I also wanted to ask him for the recipe for a cocktail that was becoming increasingly popular with the wives in Boca.

I was positive that the wonderful combination of arsenic and Dr Pepper would come in handy one day.

CPSIA information can be obtained at www.ICGtesting.com
Printed in the USA
LVOW06s1847151115

462668LV00029B/1325/P